Beyond

The

WorkPlace

How To Impact The Community Using Your Passion And Career Skills

Charlotte,
I am proud to work with you here at LCL
Happy Reading.
Ade
27/01/2021

AKINOLA IDOWU ADEWUNMI

First Published in the United Kingdom in 2020
Independent Publishing Network

Paperback – ISBN 978-1-83853-735-7

eBook – ISBN 978-1-83853-734-0

British Library's Cataloguing in Publication Data

A record of this book is available from the British
Library.

Dedication

This book is dedicated to all blood donors in Liverpool-UK, most especially blood donors from Black, Asian, and Minority Ethnic (BAME) communities who are already saving lives and those who will sign up later in the future.

CONTENTS

Contents

☞ What Is Biomedical Science?

☞ My Daily Workplace Journal

☞ How To Become A Biomedical Scientist

☞ Biomedical Science Career Prospects

Chapter Seven: Insights from My Social Action Projects

☞ Sickle Cell Disease Awareness Campaign

☞ Hospital Outreach To Africa

☞ Children's Hospital Christmas Visit

☞ STEM Ambassador Volunteering

☞ Hospital Chaplaincy Volunteering

☞ Blood Donation Campaign

Chapter Eight: When Would You Start Your Own Community Project / NGO?

☞ Start Now: Your Community Is Waiting For You

☞ What Will Be Your Legacy?

☞ Conclusion

Reference

Acknowledgements

To my lovely wife; Olubukola

Writing a book manuscript is not all that easy, without your inspirations, motivations, and encouragement I would never have been able to finish writing this book. Thank you dear for your support all the way through

To my wonderful children; Ayomide, Olamide, and Olumide

Thank you for cheering me up day and night until I finished writing this book.

To all my amazing workplace colleagues in **Haematology** and Blood Transfusion Laboratory Department, Liverpool University Hospitals NHS Foundation Trust, UK

I would like to express my deep and sincere

gratitude for your massive support. Most especially, I would like to mention and thank Charlotte Mosby and Megan Cartwright for contributing to the writing of this book.

Finally, I would like to appreciate and thank all my amazing friends, families, and everyone in my life including different community groups and faith-based organizations for all your encouragement and the support I received in various ways towards my project initiatives.

Foreword

I first met *Akinola Idowu Adewunmi* at an African Exhibition in 2018, where he attended as a blood donor ambassador, promoting blood donation awareness, particularly within the African diaspora communities across the city of Liverpool, UK. I attended the event in my role as Chairman of the Liverpool Commonwealth Association.

Since then I have got to know Akinola quite well and learn more about his passion for community service beyond his professional career as a biomedical scientist who specialises in Haematology and Blood Transfusion, with a keen research interest in Malaria and Sickle Cell Disease.

I welcome his first book, "Beyond The Workplace: How To Impact The Community Using Your Passion And Career Skills" which is indeed quite timely.

Over recent times the world has been affected by significant economic, technological, and demographic changes, wracked by endless economically-based crises, including ecological destruction and climate change, ongoing global financial crises, persistent poverty, gender and racial-ethnic inequality amidst abundance - all leading to endless discussions on the essence of work and the collective responsibilities of all humans to each other in advancing social well-being in our societies.

The book informs readers that the essence of work is fulfilling our life's purpose. People who think that work is just occupation and a place to get what you want - money, time off, and benefits – will not achieve fulfilment. According to Maslow's hierarchy of needs, growth needs do not stem from a lack of something, but rather from a desire to grow as a person. Once these growth needs have been reasonably satisfied, one may be able to reach the highest level called self-actualisation. The focus of working is not only to receive money but also to give and provide service to others. Readers are encouraged to adopt this attitude, and the author believes they will surely achieve authentic success regardless of what kind of job they have.

The essence of work is about systems alignment. **Are your physical needs, your emotional needs, your mental needs, and your spiritual needs being aligned? The book provides practical solutions to aid you in answering these questions.**

This book artfully walks the reader through the steps for serving others and communities beyond their workplaces or career. Quite significantly it presents examples of the author's own extensive "Social Action Projects", through various transformational activities in the field of education, business, community cohesion, health, and well-being.

Never has a collective sense of solidarity been more important in our societies. It is an awareness of our shared interests, objectives, standards, and sympathies creating a psychological sense of unity and interconnectivity. It refers to the ties in a society that bind people together as one.

This book is for anyone who truly wishes to understand the real purpose of work and how they can make a difference in their communities and the world - with desire, drive, dedication, discipline, passion, and persistence.
After all, we are all connected...

"In lowliness of mind let each esteems others better than himself. Let each of you look out not only for his own interests, but also for the interests of others."

Garth Orlando Dallas MBA, LLM, FRSA

Internationally renowned Legal and Business Consultant.

Chairman, Liverpool Commonwealth Association

https://liverpoolcommonwealth.org

Introduction

"Life's most persistent and urgent question is, what are you doing for others?"

-Dr. Martin Luther King Jr.

We live in a world in which people wake up every day and hurry to work. The majority of people are in a struggle for survival, they work 9-5 every day of the week only because they need money to survive. Not too many people understand the essence and value of work and as a result, abuse it. Most people work only to get money, cars, houses, and all other material wealth for themselves. Many do not understand that there is more to work than just earning salaries. They do not care about the problems and needs in their communities nor how to solve them.

In a world of so much egocentrism as ours, there is a need to shift our focus from self and pay attention to the needs of others, the problems of society, and how we can solve them. It is for these reasons that I have written this book to explain the essence of work, the reason for the workplace, and how we can extend our work skills beyond the workplace and use them to impact society.

What are you doing to help others? What and when would you give back to your community? If you have been longing to do something for others outside of your workplace or career and you don't know how to start, then this book will be valuable for you. You will learn how to use your career skills, social skills, ethical skills, general life skills, and your passion to create social action projects that will positively transform your immediate community and the nation. If you are already running your community project or doing something for others, you will also find this book useful as you will gain some insights and inspirations from the stories of other change-makers that will motivate you to take your project to the next level.

While work is a good tool for earning a living, we must also learn to go beyond our workplaces to effect a change in our communities. You and I were created for impact and we must impact our communities and nations with everything we've got. However, to impact the community, we must first learn to impact our workplaces and acquire the necessary skills with which we can serve mankind. If we can do excellent work at our workplaces, then we can replicate such excellent work in our communities.

Impacting the community starts from your workplace when you do your job very well; and extends to the society where you use your work skills to fix societal problems.

Chapter One

Understanding the Workplace

Chapter One

Understanding the Workplace

All over the world, innumerable numbers of people wake up every morning, get ready, and head to their workplaces. What do they seek to achieve? To work, averagely for 7.5 hours per day and return home. The routine continues each day for one month and another cycle begins the following month.

There are several reasons for which people go to the workplace and make working a crucial part of their lives; some to earn a living, others to stay employed, and a few more to just get busy after university. Whatever the case may be, the deplorable state of our world today is proof of the fact that the majority of people who go to work every day do not have a robust understanding of the meaning and essence of work or the workplace. It is for this reason that I have decided to explain in this book the purpose of the workplace and the essence of work.

Place of Primary Assignment

If I were to ask you these questions what would your response be? What is the purpose of the workplace? What is the essence of work? Why do you wake up every morning and get ready to hurry up to your workplace? Why do you give an average of 7.5 hours daily or 37.5 hours a week of your life to your job?

Perhaps, you may not have sat down to think about any of these questions. You probably may have been busy working but hardly ever thought of the essence of work. Maybe, just like most people, you are too engrossed with the desire to just survive that you do not care to know about the essence of work as long as you get some change to pay your bills and make ends meet monthly. Whatever category you may fall into, it doesn't matter.

I understand that we live in a world that is structured in such a way as to condition us to just follow the status quo and the routines without asking why. We have evolved a human race that does what the generation before us did without knowing why we should do the same or if we should do something else. "Our fathers worked to make ends meet, so we must also work to make ends meet" has become humanity's tacit slogan.

Be that as it may, I would like to state here that there is something about work that is beyond survival and beyond just having a workplace. Until we understand the purpose of work, we would perpetually abuse it and the consequence of that abuse would be evident in the deplorable state of our world.

The first thing I would like you to know is that the workplace is not just a place to go earn a living as most people think, but a place of primary assignment. Yes! It is a place of primary assignment. Every one of us has been given an assignment to carry out on the earth and for most people; the workplace is the place for carrying out that assignment. You would never maximize your workplace if you do not first find out if your primary assignment on the earth is tied to it. I believe that if you discover the purpose of your life today and that your current workplace is the exact location you should be carrying out your primary assignment, your attitude to work would change. You would no longer work because you need money to survive but because you want to fulfill your life's mission.

If the workplace is not just a place to earn money to meet basic needs but a place of primary assignment, how then should we approach work to fulfill its true essence? To achieve this, to maximize the purpose of work, every one of us must cultivate an attitude of service rather than just focusing on the salary that comes to us at the end of the day.

The number one proof that a person has an understanding of the workplace and the essence of work is his attitude to service. It does not matter whether you work as a doctor at the hospital or work in a school as a teacher, one thing is true; you were employed to serve. Your workplace is your place of rendering service; and service to humanity is your primary assignment on the earth. Unless we understand this truth, we would take for granted the unique opportunity and privilege that we have to be a blessing to the world and we would do our work haphazardly without commitment.

"To accomplish its purpose, work cannot be reduced to a mere means of satisfying wants and needs. It must find constant expression in service to humanity. When performed in a spirit of service, work may be seen as an act of worship".

-Bahá'u'lláh

In the words of Bahá'u'lláh as quoted above, I find something striking that I would love to draw your attention to. That is the fact that *work may be seen as an act of worship.* Wow! Worship? How could work be an act of worship when we are just working to get a paycheque to meet our needs? That is the question that most people would ask if they were told that they ought to see work as a form of worship. Worship involves devotion, commitment, faithfulness, and reverence and if we could approach work from this point of view, we would turn our cosmos into paradise before we realize it.

When the Jewish Apostle, Paul first wrote to the citizens of Colossae, one of the interesting portions of his letters that caught my attention was:

"Whatever you do, work at it with all your heart, as working for the Lord, not for human masters, since you know that you will receive an inheritance from the Lord as a reward. It is the Lord Christ you are serving" -Apostle Paul, The Bible

What exactly was Paul saying? He was saying the same thing that I have already stated earlier; the fact that work ought to be done with a heart of service as though we were worshiping God. It simply means that you and I must begin to see work as a mission, as an assignment for which we would receive eternal rewards.

Would you still approach your work haphazardly if you knew you would receive eternal rewards beyond your monthly salary? How committed would you be to your workplace if you knew that you were on a mission to serve not just humans but to worship a deity?

How would your work ethic change if you saw work as an act of worship? Unfortunately, in many developing and religious countries, many people abandon their workplaces to go and seek God in the temple for worship. They leave their workshops, laboratories, hospitals, courtrooms, etc where they should be rendering services to humanity. If only they knew that God is so much interested in the services we provide to our fellow humans at our different workplaces than going to the temple for worship.   If only they knew that they could make their works, their worship, and their workplaces, their temples. If we could give such devotion, commitment, and concentration to our works as we give to God when we want to pray and sing songs of worship, we would turn our nations around for good. All effort and exertion put forth by man from the fullness of his heart is worship, if it is prompted by the highest motives and the will to do service to humanity. This is worship "to serve mankind and to minister to the needs of the people."[1]

I believe that God gets more worship when you as a surgeon excise that cancerous lump from the body of your sick patients and restore their health than leaving your job when you ought to be at your workplace for going to a temple for worship.

I believe that God would be more pleased if you as a research scientist would invest more of your time in the laboratory to find the cure to the numerous diseases destroying the bodies of your fellow humans than spending all your time praying and dancing at a religious meeting.

It doesn't matter what your area of specialization is, be it medicine, engineering, education, security, etc. What matters is that you do your work with such a spirit of service and an attitude of worship that will create a lasting impact on your society and nation.

But what do we see happening in our societies today? We see patients dying from doctors' negligence and lack of commitment. We see decay in our educational system for lack of teachers and lecturers' devotion to their jobs and still get their wages at the end of the day. How many people die daily in our communities due to the failure of our security servicemen to take their jobs seriously? I could go on listing how endangered our world has become simply because we failed to understand the purpose of work. I could go ahead and tell you how many people die daily just because of our misconceptions about work being just a means to make ends meet.

Our failure to realize that work is our primary assignment, our mission and our life's purpose has done a lot more damage to our world than we could imagine.

Dear reader, you are on a mission, you were created to fulfill an assignment, and the only way to accomplish that is through work. Work is not a mere means of satisfying wants and needs, and the earlier we realize that the better our world would be. Work is a call to service, a call to worship divinity by serving humanity. If you and I must see work from this perspective, then we must be ready to do it with all our hearts, with commitment, devotion, and excellence, knowing that beyond the salaries, there are eternal rewards for painstakingly serving our fellow humans and making the world a better place. Your workplace is your place of primary assignment and it requires excellence.

Career Excellence

The only way to positively impact society and make life better for all humans is through work. I would, therefore, argue that, for you to maximally impact the workplace or society and become a sought-after personality; you must strive for excellence in your work or field of endeavor. It is not enough to just have a job and go to work every day, one must become excellent in what one does if one desires to make any reasonable impact. Your quality of service depends on your level of excellence. It does not matter whether you work as a vehicle mechanic, as a cleaner, or as a manager at Microsoft, without excellence, it is impossible to make a difference in your world.

Why do you need to be excellent at what you do? There are several reasons. The first thing I would like you to know in this regard is that the quality of service or impact you can render to people is a product of your excellence. The more excellent you are at your workplace, the more impact you make. Secondly, most workplace managers recognize excellence when they see it and if you are excellent at your job, you would be recognized and promoted. Most people in workplaces dream or desire of getting promoted but a lot of them remain in the same position for a very long time because they lack the excellence and professional skills required for the promotion.

In all areas of life, you would find people whose dream is to become the best and reach the zenith of their professions.

However, that doesn't happen because most of the people who aspire to reach the height of their careers fail to pursue excellence. When you do a shabby job and work haphazardly, nobody would promote you. Excellence is a promoter.

Thirdly, excellent work announces you to your world beyond your workplace. When you are excellent at what you do, you are elevated by your excellent work and the great people of society would look for you. Your excellent work will bring you before kings!

Benjamin Franklin (1706-1790), one of the leading figures of early American history was a statesman, author, publisher, scientist, inventor, and diplomat. He wrote in his autobiography about the importance of diligence and excellence at work and I am going to share that with you. People who write autobiographies usually have an agenda in mind, and Benjamin Franklin's agenda is fairly obvious. He told the story of his own life to provide an example to young people starting their careers. Franklin was saying: here are the lessons that I have learned; here are the keys to my success. One of those keys was a particular word of encouragement that Franklin took from the Bible, from a verse in the Old Testament. When Franklin was a boy, his father would often quote to him the following proverb from Solomon:

"Do you see a man skilled in his work? He will stand before kings; He will not stand

before obscure men."

-King Solomon, The Bible

Writing in his autobiography, Benjamin Franklin recalled that he took seriously his father's admonition. From his youth onward, he considered skilled work to be a pathway to fortune and fame. Now, he did not expect that he would ever literally stand before kings. And yet, as he later pointed out, that was exactly what happened. As he said in his autobiography, "I have stood before five kings and even had the honor of sitting down with the King of Denmark to dine."[2]

Benjamin Franklin indeed stood before kings in his days and it was because he understood the value of excellence at work. More than 200 years after his death, Franklin remains one of the most celebrated figures in U.S. history. His image appears on the $100 bill, towns, schools, and businesses across America are named after him.[3]

Benjamin Franklin is just one of many great

people who got to the top of their careers through excellence. Time would fail me to mention Dr. Ben Carson, Dr. Myles Munroe, Lionel Messi, etc.

Coach said, "the quality of a man's life is in direct proportion to his commitment to excellence, regardless of his chosen field of endeavor"-Sherman Alexie

The fourth thing you need to know about excellence is that it makes you a better person, a more skillful person, and a professional. Striving for excellence is one of the most important aspects of professionalism. No one can truly become professional in his or her chosen area without striving for excellence. When you go after excellence, your focus is not on the salary or finances, even though that must be expected too. Your focus is on putting quality in everything you do. A man of excellence tends to dedicate himself to giving his best into whatever he does. He sees his work as his signature. He puts a stamp of excellence by his integrity into whatever he does.[4]

It doesn't matter what your area of career is. You need to be excellent at what you do. Your workplace would only feel your impact if you do an excellent job. A look at history reveals that through excellence one can become a household name, a name that lives on for many generations even after its bearer is long gone. We could say that men of excellence live forever. Though they die, their legacies live on, their impacts are still felt in a world in which they are no longer physically present and their names never leave the lips of generations after them. Such men of excellence work not because they are after money but because they understand work as an act of service, a way of worship, and as a primary assignment.

When you hear names like Michelangelo, Beethoven, and Shakespeare, excellence comes to mind, their impacts come to mind. These men served their generations through their works and many years after they are gone, the world still talks about them. How excellent are you at your workplace? What will your generation and generations after you say about your work? What will they remember you for? Martin Luther King Junior is quoted to have said:

"If a man is called to be a street sweeper, he should sweep streets even as a Michaelangelo painted, or Beethoven composed music or Shakespeare wrote poetry. He should sweep streets so well that all the hosts of heaven and earth will pause to say, 'Here lived a great street sweeper who did his job well." -Martin Luther King Jr.

From the foregoing, we see that it doesn't matter what your area of calling or career is, what matters is your ability to do excellent work that will impact society and make the world a better place. If you are called to be a street sweeper, sweep excellently! If you are called to be a painter, paint excellently! If you are called to be a musician, play and sing excellently! If you are called to be a teacher, teach excellently! If you are called to be a doctor, treat and care for your patients excellently! If you are called to be an architect, do an excellent job! Whatever you are called to do, do it excellently, not because you need money to survive but because you want to serve humanity and make the world a better place.

Impact Beyond Your Workplace

Before bringing this chapter to a close, I would like to state that while it is good to make an impact at our workplaces where we earn a living, we must think outside the box and not limit our impacts to the four walls of our workplaces. Our career`s expertise and skills must be used to care for others and make our communities better. Of what value are your work skills if the people in your community are deprived of those skills daily and die for lack of impactful service? What good have you done if you earn millions working as an excellent doctor in your workplace while the people in your immediate neighbourhood die from preventable and curable diseases because they lack the wherewithal to afford medical care? It does not matter how skillful or how wealthy you are, until that skill and wealth can serve the most deprived members of society who cannot pay you for your work, you have not lived to serve humanity's interest but your pocket.

The goal of this book is not only to encourage you to impact your workplace but also to inspire you to take that impact beyond your workplace into the communities, the poor neighbourhood who cannot pay for your services, and to the down and out of society. If the purpose of work is not to merely satisfy our wants and needs but to serve humanity, we can only prove that by rendering our services to people who are outside our workplaces without expecting anything in return from them.

Just recently, a high school student was found

giving free haircuts and food to the homeless in South Florida. 18-year-old Joshua Rodriguez went into Miami's Overtown neighbourhood on a Sunday with a desire to help. Rodriguez said he has been cutting hair for two years, and decided he wanted to help those in need.

The high school senior and his friend, Bruno Diaz, spent $200 on food and daily essentials to offer people in the area. The two set up a table with snacks and water under an overpass and had anyone who wanted a free haircut sit down in Rodriguez's makeshift barber chair. "If you have a talent or gift then you can put it to use to help other people," Rodriguez wrote. "It's an act that often takes more selflessness and good intention than it does money." The teens later started their own non-profit, called "Blessed 2 Bless Others"[5]

From the above, we could see that irrespective of our area of specialization, we could use our skills and proficiency outside our workplaces to serve our communities and nations for no financial gains. Only when we learn to use our expertise to serve people beyond our workplaces that we can truly say we have fulfilled the purpose of work; "to serve mankind and to minister to the needs of the people".

I am going to share with you the story of a doctor who took his career excellence and skills beyond his workplace across two continents to offer selfless service to mankind.

Neurosurgeons are known to be skilled operators, but straddling surgeries across two continents? That's a different skill entirely.

Dr. Olawale Sulaiman, 49, is a professor of neurosurgery and spinal surgery, chairman of the neurosurgery department, and also chairman of the back and spine center at the Ochsner Neuroscience Institute in New Orleans. He lives in Louisiana, but splits his time between the US and Nigeria in Africa, spending up to 12 days each month providing healthcare in the country of his birth- sometimes for free.

Born in Lagos Island, Lagos, Nigeria, Sulaiman says his motivation comes from growing up in a relatively poor region.

"I am one of 10 children born into a polygamous family. My siblings and I shared one room where we often found ourselves sleeping on a mat on the floor," he told CNN. His parents could not afford his university tuition, but Sulaiman said at the age of 19, he received a scholarship to study medicine in Bulgaria through the Bureau for External Aid, a Nigerian government program targeted at improving the quality of life for Nigeria's most vulnerable communities.

Sulaiman said the scholarship opened many doors and in turn, he feels responsible to give back through healthcare. "Africans who have had the privilege of getting outstanding training and education abroad must mobilize their network of influence to transform our continent," he said. According to a report by the Global Health Workforce Alliance, Nigeria's healthcare system does not have enough personnel to effectively deliver essential health services to the country's large population.

Sulaiman says he wants to use his knowledge to improve the healthcare system. "As I often do, I consulted with my loving and devoted wife for advice. We both decided that giving back was the only option for both of us and our family. We have never looked back," he added.

In 2010, Sulaiman established RNZ Global, a healthcare development company with his wife, Patricia. The company provides medical services including neuro and spinal surgery and also offers health courses like first aid CPR in Nigeria and the US.

Noting a shortfall in physician-scientists (doctors with a combined degree in medicine and a Ph.D.) like himself, Sulaiman decided it was important to extend his expertise to Nigeria too.

"I would use my vacation times for the

medical missions, which were also planned with education and training sessions. We donated a lot of medications, equipment, and hands-on training on surgical techniques," he said.

Sulaiman said he negotiated a 25% pay cut with his American employer in exchange for longer holidays to Nigeria to pursue his passion. RNZ Global has treated more than 500 patients and provided preventative medicines for up to 5,000 people in the US and Nigeria.

Dr. Yusuf Salman, a neurosurgeon based in Abuja, Nigeria has known Sulaiman since 2006. In 2013, through a partnership with MPAC, a faith-related organization, both doctors worked together to provide free spinal surgeries to underprivileged Nigerians in Kwara, north-central Nigeria.

"(Sulaiman) came to Nigeria with implants and equipment from the US so that we could operate for free on people with spine-related problems. He was the head surgeon, a couple of others and I assisted him at the time. We did about 10 surgeries," Salman said.

RNZ Global also has a not-for-profit arm called RNZ foundation. The foundation, registered in 2019, focuses on managing patients with neurological diseases for free.

"We offer free services and surgeries for those that are less privileged and cannot afford the cost," said Blessing Holison, patient care coordinator for RNZ Global. Sulaiman hopes to establish at least four neuroscience centers in Nigeria in the coming years.[6]

Why did I share this story with you? It is to encourage you to take your skills beyond your workplace into the communities where the helpless, the needy, and the poor can be impacted by it. You do not have to be a doctor to impact your community. You could be a tailor, taxi driver, teacher, barber, pharmacist, etc but still, take your expertise beyond your workplace to the people who cannot afford to pay you and impact them selflessly. That is service, that is worship, that is the mission and your primary assignment.

"The best way to find yourself is to lose yourself in the service of others" -Mahatma Gandhi

Remember that the purpose of work is not to merely enrich oneself at the expense of others, but to render selfless service to all mankind and make the world a better place. Your impact beyond the workplace will give you greater sense of purpose, true happiness, and life fulfillment.

Nuggets One

☞ The deplorable state of our world today
  is proof of the fact that the majority of
  people who go to work every day do not
  have a robust understanding of the
  meaning and essence of work or the
  workplace.

☞ We live in a world that is structured in
  such a way as to condition us to just
  follow the status quo and the routines
  without asking why.

☞ Until we understand the purpose of
  work, we would perpetually abuse it and
  the consequence of that abuse would be
  evident in the deplorable state of our
  world.

☞ Every one of us has been given an
  assignment to carry out on the earth and
  for most people; the workplace is the
  place for carrying out that assignment.

☞ You would never maximize your
  workplace if you do not first find out

whether your primary assignment on the earth is tied to it.

☞ To maximize the purpose of work, every one of us must cultivate an attitude of service rather than just focusing on the salary that comes to us at the end of the day.

☞ The number one proof that a person has an understanding of the workplace and the essence of work is his attitude to service. It does not matter whether you work as a doctor at the hospital or work in a school as a teacher, one thing is true; you were employed to serve.

☞ God is so much interested in the services we provide to our fellow humans at our different workplaces than going to the temple for worship.

☞ Make your work your worship and your workplace, your temple.

☞ It doesn't matter what your area of specialization is, be it medicine, engineering, education, security, etc. What matters is that you do your work with such a spirit of service and an attitude of worship that will create a lasting impact on your society and nation.

☞ Our failure to realize that work is our primary assignment, our mission, and our life's purpose has done a lot more damage to our world than we could imagine.

☞ It does not matter whether you work as a vehicle mechanic, as a cleaner, or as a manager at Microsoft, without excellence, it is impossible to make a difference in your world.

☞ It does not matter how skillful or how wealthy you are, until that skill and wealth can serve the most deprived members of society who cannot pay you for your work, you have not lived to serve humanity's interest but your pocket.

☞ Only when we learn to use our expertise to serve people beyond our workplaces that we can truly say we have fulfilled the purpose of work; "to serve mankind and to minister to the needs of the people.

☞ Impacting the community starts from your workplace when you do your job very well, and extends to the society where you use your work skills to fix societal problems.

☞ Your impact beyond the workplace will give you greater sense of purpose, true happiness, and a life of fulfillment.

Chapter Two

Social Action and Your Community

Chapter Two

Social Action and Your Community

"The greatness of a community is most accurately measured by the compassionate actions of its members"

– Coretta Scott King

In this chapter, we shall discuss the concept of social action and how it relates to your community.

What is Social Action?

Social action is an organized program of socioeconomic reform as defined by the Merriam Webster dictionary. There are few other quality definitions like; Social action is about people coming together to help improve their lives and solve problems that are important in their communities[1]. I will also say that social action is when individuals identify an issue or problem in our local, national, or international communities and then take action to address it. It's a strategy for community development, and a powerful tool to create positive change. We must all therefore embrace and practice the concept of social action.

Ways Of Doing Social Action

To develop societies and enhance deprived communities, we must all engage in some form of social action to bring reformation to all aspects of humanity. Such social actions will require us to look beyond our workplaces into areas of society that are often neglected and feel the least impact of our workplaces. Most people usually do not notice neglected and deprived communities. They are too busy trying to earn a living that it never occurs to them that there are neighbourhoods that are deprived of the necessities of life like food, water, healthcare, etc.

Others are attentive enough to notice the

problems in their surroundings but instead of taking action to remedy them, they resort to playing the blame game. They complain and blame the government for the deplorable state of things or accuse the rich of abandoning the poor. They do not take any action to alleviate the plight of the people. They are rather concerned about how much money they would make at the end of the month to take care of themselves and their immediate families. They are not community-focused and hence stop at complaining without actions. The tragedy of this age is that people are too self-centered and care only about their wellbeing. The result of such self-centeredness is that everyone stands by and watches the poor and deprived of society die in lack and penury. Everyone sees the problem but no one is selfless enough to take action to solve it.

What then should be our disposition in such instances? What should we do when we notice societal problems? We ought to solve them through social actions. Nothing changes until we take action. Our skills and expertise at our workplaces ought to be brought into such needy communities to solve the existing problems free of charge if possible. This is what social action is all about.

 The question most people usually ask is "how can we do social action?" That may perhaps be your question too. You may have seen an area of interest where you would like to help, improve a situation, and solve a societal problem but do not know how to go about it. There are a lot of people just like you facing the same challenge; the challenge of how to start. You may not even have the means to solve the problems that you have noticed and have a desire to change. That shouldn't deter you at all. You do not have to be a millionaire to start a social action project. All you need is the skill, willingness, passion to help, and knowledge of how to implement that social action. I am going to share with you several ways by which you could start a social action and fulfill your dreams of bringing solutions to the prevailing problems of society.

So how can social action be done? Social action can be done of which the primary aim is to address societal problems through many ways including volunteering, community development programs, advocacy/campaigning, fundraising activities, and social enterprise services which involve setting up non-profit businesses or organizations through which you can use your workplace skills and experience to bring reforms to your community. In addition to the above, any other practical actions you can think of in the service of others including helping the destitute or providing a service to complement the public services to make a difference can be your social action.

Volunteering: This is the use of your time and skills freely to benefit others and your community. For example, during the Covid-19 pandemic, the UK government was looking for up to 250,000 volunteers from different professional backgrounds to support the health system-National Health Service (NHS) and other care sectors to tackle the overwhelming COVID-19 health crisis. Surprisingly, more than 750, 000 people responded to this national call "Your NHS needs you". What a great way of demonstrating community spirit and social solidarity!

Look around the communities where you live and work; there are numerous volunteering opportunities where you can use the combination of your career skills, time, and passion to make a meaningful difference.

Community development: This is about joining your efforts or providing resources together with other members of your community to collectively take action to develop the community or to fix common problems. For example, collective social action can be taken by you and other members of your community for projects like; Building a house for the homeless people or Fighting community crime.

Social enterprise: This is about setting up a not-for-profit organization or business for the interest of the people or community. You can set up a business with social objectives and use your workplace experiences or career skills to benefit the underprivileged or you can set up a community interest organization to champion a good cause that you are passionate about. This is exactly what Louise Goulden did. She founded "The Together Project", a social enterprise with a mission to reduce loneliness, improve wellbeing, tackle ageism and help integrate local communities.

Advocacy/Campaigning: This is about working with decision-makers to raise awareness or to campaign for social justice/social change/social impact. For example; you can start a petition to effect change on any social ills that are close to your heart and get people to sign it. You can advocate for a policy change to address community problems. You can get involved in politics to effect change. You can start an awareness campaign project to educate people on a subject you are passionate about to effect change, for example, domestic violence or disease prevention

Fundraising: This is using your platform, influence, or personal profile to fundraise for a good cause in your community. The inspirational story of Captain Sir Thomas Moore, popularly known as "Captain Tom" will linger in the minds of thousands of British people for years to come. In the UK during the Covid-19 pandemic, Captain Tom, a 99-year-old war veteran used his personal profile to start a fundraising campaign. He originally aimed to raise just £1,000 for the NHS by setting a goal for himself to walk the 25 meters around his garden 100 times over several days, ahead of his 100th birthday.

He received massive support and donations from a lot of inspired donors both in the UK and around the world during and after reaching his goal of walking 100 times. He eventually raised over £30 million for the NHS and other care sectors. What a small way to make a big difference! Everyone has got a platform; everyone has influence; use yours to benefit others without expecting anything in return.

Another example of social action through fundraising was done by Jeanette Höglund. She is the founder and CEO of By Your Side (Vid Din Sida) based in Stockholm, Sweden.

By Your Side is a Swedish non-profit organization, founded by Jeanette Höglund who used to work for Stockholm Public Transport Security. After years of witnessing an alarming number of homeless people, Jeanette decided she had to do something to address the problem. She started by doing a live broadcast on social media, asking her friends to help her donate so she could provide these people with clothing, food, and hygiene products. In the first week, they raised 35, 000 Swedish Krona (around £3,000). Today the organization has grown and is funded by volunteers, private donations, and collections.[2] Apart from the aforementioned examples of social action projects, I will also use my life's story and that of others as examples of how we can all take social action to every community that has been deprived of real development.

Some years ago, my wife and I were so passionate about doing something to help others. After we were inspired to start helping sick people, we had to take action by starting a social action project. We founded PathLab Support, a social enterprise in April 2012 out of compassion to support the sick, most especially individuals and families affected with Sickle Cell Disease in the UK and Africa. From that time till now, we have been helping and supporting sick children and their families. I will share with you the details of this project in the later chapter.

Social action projects can be done by anyone and in any field of life. All you need to start is compassion to identify a problem and think of ways to solve it. That was exactly what

Maureen Muketha did. Maureen Muketha is a 25 years old trained nutritionist and founder of Tule Vyema in Kenya. When she saw that there was a need in her community related to malnutrition and poor eating habits, she decided to take her professional skills from the workplace to the streets to solve the problem of malnutrition ravaging her community. She decided to use her passion and career skills for social impact. What did she do?

She founded a Community Based Organization called Tule Vyema. A Swahili word for "Let's Eat Right". The organization raises awareness of proper nutrition practices in communities to eliminate incidences of malnutrition.

Tule Vyema engages communities through information sessions and teaching young, unemployed women to cultivate indigenous vegetables in sacks (sack farming) for both their consumption and sale of surplus to meet their other household needs[3]

Over 400 households around Kiserian in Kajiado County, Kenya have been made food secured, improving their nutrition status, and economically empowering them. Additionally, Tule Vyema conducts regular deworming drives for children under the age of 12 to eliminate helminths that would otherwise cause iron deficiency anemia, poor appetite, diarrhea, and other incidences of morbidity that are detrimental to their health. They have dewormed over 1,200 children till date.[4]

What an inspiring story! Just like Maureen we all must learn to excel at our professions beyond the workplace, go to the streets, the neighbourhoods, the needy communities, and impact them with our work skills and professional knowledge. You have and possess the skills that can benefit your community. What is the use of being a nutritionist when all the children in your neighbourhood are suffering from malnutrition-related ailments? What is the use of being a skilled tailor or fashion designer when the poor kids in your community walk around with torn clothes? Why are you a teacher when the underprivileged children in your community are deprived of education?

Whatever skills you have, whatever your profession is, if your community does not benefit from it, it is only of little value. If you only work for the money, then you have not yet understood the purpose of work. The purpose of work is to serve mankind and make our world better. The only way to serve mankind and better our world with our skills selflessly is through social actions. I implore you to look around your community, find a need, and meet it.

"True greatness, true leadership, is achieved not by reducing men to one's service but in giving oneself in selfless service to them" -J. Oswald Sanders

Understanding Your Community

Community impact is the positive difference you make for a good cause you are passionate about. It involves solving problems and making life better for the people in the community. However, to be a successful changemaker, it is required of you to first know and understand your community. How then can you understand your community? You must first understand the meaning of community.

A community is a group of people who share something in common.[5]

Therefore a community could be where you live-your local community; where you work-your workplace community; or if defined by culture-e.g. African community; by profession-Biomedical Science community; by the religion-Christian community; or by city/place-Liverpool community; or by organization-Liverpool Clinical Laboratories (LCL) community.

The group of people in a community also cares about what they have in common, about each other, and their geographical locations.

From the above, it is obvious that the community is more about people; that is why we all belong to multiple and overlapping communities based on what we share in common. So whenever you think about a community, think also about the healthy relationships that exist among people from different backgrounds. The description of a community will, of course, include the geographical locations, neighbourhoods, physical features, economic ties, and the surrounding environments.

Each community is therefore different, based on the cultures, religions, ethnicity, language, and core values or interest. Now that you can identify different types of communities, it behoves you to make a difference in any of these communities. However, to know how to impact any particular community, you must first understand that community. How would you make a difference if you do not know and understand your community settings, the people you want to help, and the social issues you want to address?

To understand your community, you need to do a little research to know about the people, demographics, cultures, history, political structure, core values, religious beliefs, social structures, and of course the problems or issues affecting people and their environments.

Reading local newspapers, visiting the local library to read historical books, attending community meetings, internet searching, and interacting with residents are few ways of getting information about your community.

Once you have done your research and identify the problems, then go ahead and solve them by creating social action projects.

Importance/Benefits Of Social Action

Are there any benefits or importance of social action? Definitely! Social action allows us to improve the lives of others and empower communities. We can eliminate the ills of society through social actions. Sicknesses and diseases can be cured through social action. Poverty can be eradicated from our communities through social action. The problem of theft, armed robbery, and fraud can be solved through social action. The problem of teenage pregnancy can be addressed through social action. Drug and substance abuse, addiction, gangsterism, etc. can be impeded in our societies through social action. The problem of homelessness and inadequate shelter can be solved through social action. The problem of rape, gender-based violence, child molestation, human trafficking, and similar vices can be solved through social action. Preventable genetic disorders like Sickle Cell Disease can be prevented through social action. The spread of STD like AIDS, Syphilis, etc can be prevented through social action. The problem of corruption, electoral fraud, Police brutality, etc. can all be solved through social action. Almost all societal problems can be solved through social action.

Furthermore, social action brings a feeling of fulfillment knowing that we are living a life of service to humanity and not just living for selfish gains. Social action in most cases enhances our skills and helps us to discover, learn, and develop new ones. The joy of meeting new friends and connecting with people for whom you owe nothing but genuine love and service also comes with social action. Finally, we become great by serving others through social action. In the end, only those who out of love, live for the service of others are truly great.

"Everybody can be great...because anybody can serve. You don't need to have a college degree to serve. You don't have to make your subject and verb agree to serve. You only need a heart full of grace. A soul generated by love"

-Martin Luther King, Jr.

How do I get social action project ideas? How

do I know where or who to help? Maybe that is the question you are asking. The answer is simple. To get a social action project idea, you need to look for the prevailing problems in your communities, think about ways to solve them, and then take practical actions. It is often the case that people only complain about the problems they see in their societies without doing anything to solve them. Instead of joining the crowd to complain about the problems that we see in our communities, we should rather create avenues for solving them. I believe that while the rest of the world passively ignores the plights of the victims of disadvantaged communities, those whose heroic souls have been taught to serve and live for the good of all mankind must step forward and effect positive change.

"Heroes are Ordinary People whose social action is Extra-Ordinary/ who ACT when others are passive, who give up EGO-centrism for SOCIO-centrism" -Philip Zimbardo

Nuggets Two

☞ To develop societies and enhance deprived communities, we must all engage in some form of social action to bring reformation to all of humanity.

☞ Most people usually do not notice neglected and deprived communities. They are too busy trying to earn a living that it never occurs to them that there are neighbourhoods that are deprived of the necessities of life like food, water, healthcare, etc.

☞ The tragedy of our age is that people are too self-centered and care only about their wellbeing. The result of such self-centeredness is that everyone stands by and watches the poor and deprived of society die in lack and penury. Everyone sees the problem but no one is selfless enough to take action to solve it.

☞ We all must learn to beyond excelling at our profession in our workplaces, go to the streets, the neighbourhoods, the needy communities, and impact them with our work skills and professional knowledge.

☞ Whatever skills you have, whatever your profession is, if your community does not benefit from it, it is only of little value.

☞ If you only work for the money, then you have not yet understood the purpose of work. The purpose of work is to serve mankind and make our world better.

☞ The only way to serve mankind and better the world with your skills selflessly is through social actions. Look around your community, find a need, and meet it.

☞ We become great by serving others through social action. In the end, only those who out of love, live for the service of others are truly great.

☞ While the rest of the world passively ignores the plights of the victims of disadvantaged communities, those whose heroic souls have been taught to serve and live for the good of all mankind must step forward and effect positive change.

☞ Work in its true purpose is for service; service to the human race, service to those who are deprived and disadvantaged in our societies.

☞ Social action is a strategy for community development, and a powerful tool to create positive change.

☞ Community impact is the positive difference you make for a good cause you are passionate about.

Chapter Three

Where is your Passion?

Chapter Three

Where is your Passion?

"Find something you're passionate about and keep tremendously interested in it" -Julia Child

In this chapter, we shall discuss the need to find one's passion and use it for the good of humanity.

Find Your Passion In Life And At Work

Every one of us has been given or has developed a passion for something. We may all look alike but our passions are different. That is why one person could walk past homeless children every day and not even notice that these children need shelter, yet another person would only need to see one homeless child and be moved with a passion to build a shelter for all homeless children and start a social action program to execute that. A person who didn't notice homeless children is perhaps passionate about out-of-school children or sexually molested children. A person may not have a passion for out-of-school children but may have a passion to fight for the fundamental human right of the oppressed in society.

So, the bottom line is that we all have a passion for a given problem that we wish to solve in society. Where is your passion? What are you passionate about? Your passion is an indication of what you should be doing with your life. Passion is a feeling of being energized for something. Work would not mean an expression of service to mankind in your view if you are not passionate about your work. You would not be devoted, or happy and committed to your work if you lack passion for it. That means that you would not strive for excellence and would eventually do haphazard jobs. The reason most people neglect their duties and perfunctorily do their jobs is a lack of passion for what they do.

I understand that there are a lot of people who go to work every day but whose passion is not in their workplace or chosen career. This is often the case because we live in a world where children are forced by their parents to study university courses which they have no passion for and live the rest of their lives working at a job that they dislike. If you are such a person, what you ought to do is find where your passion is and focus on it. Use your passion for community development or to serve humanity if your job is not connected to your passion. It is better to find joy following your passion than living the rest of your life depressed at a job that you dislike. If you understand that the essence of work is not to get money but to serve, you would do everything to find and develop your passion at work even if it doesn't give you instant financial rewards. True joy and peace of mind come from doing what you love, not from doing what you dislike just to get money.

"Never work just for money or for power.

They won't save your soul or help you sleep at night." -*Marian Wright Edelman*

Live Your Passion, It Is Linked To Your Purpose

Why is it important that we all discover our passion and pursue it? The answer is simple. It is often the case that your life's passion is linked to your life's purpose, and failure to pursue that passion would result in living a purposeless and meaningless life. Your passion is linked to the reason you exist. That drive, desire, obsession about the problems you notice in the society for which you want to bring solutions is your passion and purpose of your existence. Your purpose is linked to your desire to solve a problem. Wherever you see a problem in society and you are compelled with a passion to bring a solution, there lies your life's purpose.

In life, there are two kinds of people; those who work all their lives for money without ever finding why they were born and those who discover their passion and purpose and dedicate their lives to it. The former grow old and die with no impact nor legacy. The latter through service, impact the world and leaves a legacy behind after death. While the former focuses on money, the latter focuses on passion, service, and purpose.

It is worthy of note that only people of passion transform society for good and make the world a better place. The rest are egocentric and care only about money and self. To solve the problems in our society and make the world a better place, we must all find our passion and maximize it.

I am going to use the story of Malala, the little girl who pursued her passion and fought for the right of the girl child to education, to buttress my point about why we must all pursue our passion and make society better through it.

On October 9th, 2012, Malala Yousafzai, a 15-year-old Pakistani female student was shot in the head and neck while traveling home on a school bus in a Taliban-run assassination attempt. Why the assassination attempt? She had kicked against the Taliban violation of the fundamental human right of the girl-child in Pakistan. The Taliban had warned that no girl child be allowed to go to school or have an education. Malala, feeling frustrated and enraged by the Taliban's attempt to strip every girl child their right to education could not stand by and watch such injustice being done in her community. She knew that was a problem that needed to be solved. While others overlooked the problem and some didn't even see it as a problem, Malala, driven with passion looked for a way to bring a solution. What did she do? She began to blog and wrote articles about the injustice and drew the world's attention to the Taliban's

One day, Yousafzai, officially targeted by Taliban as "promoting secularism," was riding home on a bus after taking an exam in Pakistan's Swat Valley. A masked Taliban gunman, upon entering the bus, shouted:

"Which one of you is Malala? Speak up; otherwise, I will shoot you all." Upon her being identified, she was shot twice. She was then flown abroad for surgery and after some time she recovered. Refusing to be deterred by the threat to her life and by the gunshot wound she sustained, Malala continued to advocate social justice for every girl child in Pakistan and all over the world.

A former British Prime Minister Gordon Brown (now the UN Special Envoy for Global Education) launched an official petition in honor of Yousafzai. In honor of continuing her work for educational rights for women. This petition has been launched "in support of what Malala fought [and will continue to fight] for". Using the slogan "I am Malala," the petition: calls on Pakistan to agree to a plan to deliver education for every child, calls on countries to outlaw discrimination against girls, and puts increased pressure on international organizations to put the world's children in school by 2015.[1]

Today, Yousafzai is well known for her education and women's rights activism because she fought for her passion; justice for all. She discovered her purpose and dedicated her life to pursue it. You and I must passionately solve the problems in our societies and by so doing make the world a better place. We must live for passion and purpose. We must enlighten people on the importance of channeling their passion for service to mankind via social action. Malala found her passion and built a social action project around it, what about you? Are you going to find your passion and serve mankind through it or you are going to only work for "the money" at a job you like or dislike?

Use Your Passion To Benefit Others

Before closing the chapter, I want to use the story of Otto Orrondam to explain how you can use your passion for social action if your career or workplace is not your passion. Every one of us must use our passion to benefit others and do it purposefully and passionately.

Otto Orondaam is a young African, born and raised in Nigeria, a country he has so much belief in. He acquired a bachelor's degree in Human Anatomy from the University of Port Harcourt in the year 2010. Otto Orondaam founded Slum2School Africa in 2012 during his national youth service as an intervention to advocate for and improve access/quality of education for disadvantaged children in slums and remote communities.

During his national youth service, Otto worked as a banker in Lagos state, Nigeria. On his way to work passing through the busy streets of Lagos, he sees a lot of children who are out of school just roaming the streets. Whenever he goes across the third mainland bridge in Lagos, he often looks down and sees a remote community called Makoko which is a slum neighbourhood with dirty oily floating water. One day he decided to visit that community only to be amazed by the realities that stared him in the face. He was shocked to see the living conditions in the slum and the number of out-of-school children living there. Thousands of children were out of school, there was no access to health facilities, they lacked sewage systems and the dwellers defecate into the floating water from which they also take a bath. Poverty in the slum is fierce and a lot more sad realities plagued the dwellers of the slum community of Makoko. Otto was challenged and seriously traumatized by what he saw. He felt so much pain to see a whole community live in such poor conditions. The next few months of his life were full of thoughts of how he could be of help to that community. He hardly could concentrate at work as he was often overwhelmed with the thoughts of how he could salvage the poor condition of the Makoko slum dwellers. His most pressing desire was to see the thousands of out-of-school children get an education. Otto has developed a passion!

One day he thought to himself that it was undeserving of him to sit in his air-conditioned banking office every day enjoying life while thousands of children are without a school in the slums of Makoko. He was moved with so much love and passion for the children but pained at the same time at their living conditions. Otto was faced with the decision of whether to continue his banking job or follow the passion God had put in his heart. It was a tough decision for him to make but thankfully he surrendered his job for his passion. He had to quit his job to pursue his passion. It was time for him to live for purpose instead of for money and selfish gains. It was time for him to sacrifice his life in service to mankind. He decided to live his life for others realizing that having a lucrative job does not give as much fulfillment and joy as living a fulfilled, purposeful, and passion-driven life. His decision to quit his job was not an easy one as he got so much pressure from his parents, friends, and even from his office. Everyone told him to remain a banker as that was a very lucrative career with a bright future for a young graduate like Otto. He, however, turned a deaf ear to all of the suggestions from the workplace, parents, friends, and relatives. He knew that was not why he was born. He realized that living for himself will not grant him the fulfillment of his passion to rescue the Makoko community.

Slum2School Africa Social Action Project

After quitting his job, Otto Orondaam went into the slum community and tried to make a few friends, and learned how to communicate in the basic Yoruba language. He spoke with the parents and some of the elders of the community about his intention to get free education to the children in the community. After many discussions, Otto launched his social action project which he named Slum2school Africa.

Slum2School Africa is a volunteer-driven social development organization operating in Africa whose vision is to transform society by empowering disadvantaged children in Slums to realize their full potential through the provision of educational scholarships, health support, and other psycho-social support.

Since its inception, Otto has worked with over 3000 young volunteers from over 25 countries to provide scholarships for children from various slums and many other children have also benefited from health and psycho-social support programs. He also led campaigns to renovate dilapidated schools in remote communities and equip slum schools with more facilities like computer rooms, libraries, and health centers.[2]

During the Covid-19 Pandemic, schools in Nigeria were shut down and students could no longer access educational materials and classes. Moved with a passion to see kids continue their education, Orondaam Otto launched a virtual academy. His charity created a virtual learning hub where children can learn from the comfort of their homes using digital technology.

Otto told CNN that 948 children from other rural and under-served communities have also been enrolled in the organization's virtual classes. The plan is to reach up to 10,000 learners by the end of the year, he said.

"We have trained Slum2school teachers, facilitators, and professional counsellors who engage them across various subjects," he told CNN.

The classes are designed to mimic classroom interactions in a traditional school setting and are billed as the first of its kind in the country and within the Sub-Saharan region, according to Slum2School.

With help from partners such as American sports channel ESPN and African food operator EatNGo, Otto says they have been able to supply tablets to 108 students.

Around 940 students have 40 teachers with laptops who oversee their learning via clusters of learning.

They also provided internet connectivity and headphones to the children, ensuring they can participate in online activities. He added that some of the subjects taught include civic education, health and sex education, and verbal reasoning as the classes aim to teach them various life skills.

There is also a strong tech focus as the students also learn networking and basic programming among other subjects.[3]

What an inspiring story of true passion and service! This is how we all ought to live our lives in the service of others. We ought to work mainly to benefit others. It won't be easy but it is worth the sacrifice. Creating a social action project requires sacrifice and devotion. It won't always be easy getting volunteers to partner with you in a cause that pays no salary. Taking Otto, for instance, we could see that working for the benefit of mankind is sacrificial and not a bed of roses. It was not easy for him and his team sailing through the waters in canoes to get children from the slums to school and back. It was not easy for them sacrificing the little money they had to buy learning materials and for the renovation of schools just so that the next generation could get an education. While a lot of his contemporaries are working in hospitals, in banks, and in the oil sector, Otto and his team are in the slums day and night trying to make sure that the children of the Makoko community are not deprived of the right to education. This is what it means to live for purpose and passion, to sacrifice comfort, self-benefit, salaries, fame, and job to help those deprived of education and health care. Otto believes that the purpose of humanity is to help lift each other and that we are all not successful if one of us isn't. That is the mindset we should all have; to lift others, to serve others, to sacrifice what we have to help others.

In the next few decades, some of the kids benefiting from the slum2school projects would become, doctors, engineers, lawyers, economists, presidents, etc. contributing to the development of our country. What would have become of them if a young man like Otto had not responded to the call to live a life of service and purpose? If he didn't choose to live the life of service, some of these kids would possibly end up as gangsters, terrorists, drug addicts, etc.

Our country needs more people who understand the essence of work. Unfortunately, people are more concerned about themselves than about the poor and less-privileged. Only a few go to school to get certificates because they want to help others. Only a few people apply for jobs because they want to serve others. If we could check the motive behind your acquiring that car, building that house, or establishing that business, we would perhaps discover that all the struggle was just for yourself and your family. You could live your whole life without never really caring about the problems in your society. You may not even realize that you perhaps have been living for self. If you are living for self then you are not living for the benefit of others.

I don't care how much salary you earn at your workplace, if part of that money is not used for the advancement and betterment of humanity, then it's all worthless. If your career skills, your wealth, houses, cars, degrees, and certificates do not alleviate the poverty of the poor and the needy or if the helpless and the homeless do not benefit from it or if the orphans are not catered for by it; then all of it is worthless.[4]

Dear reader, we can make our world better if we all decide to live for our passion and convert our passion into our work. If you are not passionate about your job, maybe it's time to find where your passion is and follow it. Work is an avenue to serve mankind and not just an avenue for egocentric gains. That is why you should turn your passion into your work by creating social action projects that would be instrumental in solving the various problems that exist in your community and country.

Nuggets Three

☞ Your passion is an indication of what you should be doing with your life.

☞ It is better to find joy following your passion than live the rest of your life depressed at a job that you dislike.

☞ True joy and peace of mind come from doing what you love, not from doing what you dislike just to get money.

☞ It is often the case that our life's passion is linked to our life's purpose and failure to pursue that passion would result in living a purposeless and meaningless life.

☞ Whenever you see a problem in society and you have a desire to bring a solution, there lies your life's purpose.

☞ Only people of passion transform society for good and make the world a better place.

☞ We can make our world better if we all decide to live for our passion and convert our passion into our work.

Chapter Four

Your Skill Sets Are Resources for Social Action

Chapter Four

<u>Your Skill Sets Are Resources for Social Action</u>

"No time is better spent than that spent in the service of your fellow man" -Bryant H. McGill

Often, people do not create social action projects because they think that they do not have the resources to do so. They believe that for one to initiate social actions, one has to have a lot of money or a specific skill. That is a huge misconception. There is no specific skill that is exclusively for social action; all skill sets can be used for social impact. In this chapter, we shall discuss how to use all available skills for social action.

A lot of people see a need in society and wish they had the skills to meet it. Concluding that they are void of such skills, they do nothing to meet the need. If you do not have a particular skill to meet a particular need, you should do an inventory of all your skills and you would find one that meets other needs. All our skills are meant to be used for serving others and meeting societal needs. Most people are ignorant of the fact that they could convert their skills into resources for driving positive change in their communities. All skills could be converted into some form of social action. Career skills, social skills, life's skills, moral/ethical skills can be used to bring reformation to society and to serve humanity.

Career Skills

"There is no greater calling than to serve your fellow men. There is no greater contribution than to help the weak. There is no greater satisfaction than to have done it well".

-Walter Reuther

Career skills are a combination of your

knowledge, skills, and experience at your workplace for a specific job role. The reason you go to your workplace every day is that you are knowledgeable in that field and through many years of experience you have developed excellent skills in delivering your job role. Such career skills though related to your workplace could be used for social action projects to develop your community and nation.

Career skills shouldn't be limited to your workplace if your community or society needs such skills and cannot afford them. Although your career skills are the source of your livelihood, they shouldn't be limited to that. They should be used to help the needy and alleviate the plights of the poor. If you are a medical doctor, your medical skills should benefit the poor people who cannot afford the cost of healthcare. If you are a computer scientist, your computer skills should be taught to teenagers in your community who are void of the means to attend a conventional computer school. You can organize a weekend computer training section as part of your social action project to empower others.

Whether you are an engineer, a tailor, business analyst, lawyer, biomedical scientist, etc. you can use your career skills to enrich the lives of others. You can take those skills beyond your workplace into the community to serve mankind selflessly. That was exactly what Helen Milner did.

Helen Louise Milner OBE is the CEO of Good Things Foundation, a digital and social inclusion charity based in the UK. Following a 30-year career in developing online education services to schools and other communities, she started using her career skills and passion to lead digital and social inclusion in the UK and beyond. Her social enterprise supports digitally and socially excluded people to improve their lives through digital technology. 'Digital technology and community actions are at the heart of everything her foundation does.'[1]

Social Skills

Apart from career skills, we could also develop our communities using our social skills. You might say "I don't have any professional career skills; hence I have nothing to offer to my community". That won't be true! We all have one skill or the other. It could be true that you lack professional career skills. However, you are not completely void of skills; you perhaps have social skills that could be instrumental to community development. Your social skills might be the only thing majority of the people in your community need to better their lives.

So what are social skills? Social skills are the skills we use to communicate, connect, and interact with each other, both verbally and non-verbally, through gestures, body language, and appearances. These skills help us to get along with other people. Respecting others, active listening, being polite, helping, sharing, being a team player, being on time, cooperating, empathy, compassion, and good manners are all examples of social skills. We need these skills in our daily lives, wherever we have people, and most especially in the workplace to maintain a healthy relationship with colleagues. Being polite is a vital social skill we must all develop for conflict resolution.

By using your social skills, you could design a social action project for the kids and teenagers in your community to teach them how to care, respect, cooperate, taking turns, sharing and help each other. Are social skills important? Yes, they are! They are the bedrock of a peaceful and progressive society. Furthermore, good social skills can help kids have a brighter future. According to a study published in the American Journal of Public Health, a child's social and emotional skills in kindergarten might be the biggest predictor of success in adulthood.

Researchers from Penn State and Duke University found that children who were better at sharing, listening, cooperating, and following the rules at age five were more likely to go to college. They also stand a better chance of being employed full-time by age 25. Children who lacked social and emotional skills were more likely to have substance abuse issues, relationship issues, and legal troubles. They were also more likely to depend on public assistance.[2]

To reduce the negative effects of a lack of social skills in our communities, we must educate our kids about the importance of having the right social skills, attitudes, and good behaviour. Through social action, we can teach children by visiting schools or organizing seminars, picnic, youth camp meeting, and conferences for kids and teenagers where they are taught about the danger and consequences of anti-social behaviour. Your social skills must be replicated in your community and the only way to do that is through social action projects.

Life Skills

Besides career and social skills, there are other life skills that you have with which you can impact society positively. The term 'Life Skills' refers to the necessary skills for participation in everyday life or the skills you need to make the most out of life. Any skill that is useful in your life can be considered a life skill.[3]

Creative and critical thinking skills, study skills, self-control, self-awareness, parenting skills, time management skills, leadership skills, decision making, good communication, interpersonal, public speaking skills, writing skills, etc. are all examples of life skills. The number of life skills we need for our day to day living is endless and that means we cannot possibly mention all of them here. The point, however, is for you to understand that you have one or more of those skills. The more you study yourself, the more life skills you would discover you have.

So what should you do with these life skills

after discovering that you have them? You should create a social action project around them for the good of society. Your life skills ought to be used to impact your community and nation. You may think that your life skills are not important and would be of no use to society. That is an erroneous thought. All life skills are valuable and whether you know it or not, some people desire those skills that you have. Some people need your life skills to make their lives better.

For example; university, college, or high school students who always find it difficult to study or pass exams would desire that someone teaches them the right way to study to enable them to excel in their academics. If you have excellent study habits and secrets to passing exams, you could build a social action project around that by forming a "Study Club" where students are inspired to study and taught the secrets to academic excellence. You never know how many people you would impact and how many destinies you would help sharpen.

Let's imagine that you have mastered time management and that has been instrumental to your career and life's success. You can turn that skill into a social action project. Whether you know it or not, some people do not know the value of time and hence squander it. As a result, they are not able to achieve anything of worth in life and are far-less productive than they should be.

Taking a look at our different societies, for example, you would realize that there are so many young people roaming the streets doing nothing and wasting time on trivial things. You would agree with me that any society full of young people idling away their time would hardly become a developed nation. How then could you use your time management life skills to better such a community? How can you help such young people? You can help transform that aspect of life by creating a movement, club, conference, etc. where the youths of such society are taught the importance of time and how to use it for productive endeavours. Using your career and life success as examples of how time management is beneficial to achieve success, you could explain to them why and how they should make judicious use of their time. The same is true if you have good leadership skills. Create a project around it and transfer those skills to others.

What about parenting skills? Yes, they too could be turned into social action projects. Parenting is one of the most difficult jobs in the world and most parents are having a hard time handling their kids. If you know some parenting secrets that have helped you raise upright and excellent children, you could create a "Parent Club" and share those secrets freely with other parents. You could as well convert those secrets and principles of parenting into a book that you could distribute to struggling parents.

Whatever life skills you have could be used to impact and serve your community and nation.

There is therefore no excuse. If you don't have career skills to share, you have social skills. If you don't have social skills, you have life skills. All skills must be used to impact others in our communities and nations and this could be done within or beyond our workplaces.

Ethical/Moral Skills

Before bringing this chapter to a close, I would briefly like to say that ethical or moral skills could also be transferable to others. It is unarguably true that there is an increasing moral decadence in most modern-day societies. Whether it's in Africa, Europe or America the fact is the same. Society is gradually losing its moral values and the consequence of that is glaringly evident. Violence has become rampant. Sexual harassment and corruption have become an everyday occurrence. Money and material well-being are priority goals for millions of people, who would easily give up their moral principles for financial gains or authority.[4]

In many nations of the world, corruption, bribery, and violence have become an everyday occurrence and unless we consciously take action to change this, we would never be able to build a great nation. Nothing destroys a nation as much as the lack of moral values. Corruption, dishonesty, fraud, violence, etc are some of the most destructive elements in any society. If you take a look at the least developed countries of the world, you would find that such moral decadence as mentioned above is prevalent.

How then do we solve the problem of moral and ethical failures in our society and nations? The answer is the same "through social action projects". You and I can solve the problem of moral decadence in our communities and nations by forming non-governmental organizations to address the issues. We must be committed to transforming our societies otherwise things will get worse. It is, however, the case that most people do not care about the ills in their society as long as they go to work every day and earn a salary. We could either bring positive change to society through social action to solve societal issues or pretend like we don't care. If we choose the latter, we would live in a broken, violent, and regressive society. If however, we choose the former; our societies would become peaceful, strong, and progressive ones where we can raise our kids and be confident that their future would be bright and successful.

Whatever you do, remember that all skills are for the betterment of society and that you and I must go beyond our workplaces to impact society and the nation.

Nuggets Four

☞ Often, people do not create social action projects because they think that they do not have the resources to do so. They believe that for one to initiate social actions, one has to have a lot of money or a specific skill. That is a huge misconception.

☞ There is no specific skill that is exclusively for social action; all skill sets can be used for social impact.

☞ All skills could be converted into some form of social action. Career skills, social skills, life's skills, moral/ethical skills can be used to bring reformation to society and to serve humanity.

☞ Career skills shouldn't be limited to your workplace if your community or society needs such skills and cannot afford them.

☞ Although your career skills are the source of your livelihood, they shouldn't be limited to that. They should be used to help the needy and alleviate the plights of the poor.

☞ To reduce the negative effects of a lack of social skills in our communities, we must educate our kids about the importance of having the right social skills and attitudes.

☞ All life skills are valuable and whether you know it or not, some people desire those skills that you have. Some people need your life skills to make their life better.

☞ Whatever life skills you have could be used to impact and serve your community and nation. There is therefore no excuse. If you don't have career skills to share, you have social skills. If you don't have social skills, you have life skills.

☞ Nothing destroys a nation as much as the lack of moral values. Corruption, bribery, dishonesty, fraud, violence, etc. are some of the most destructive elements in any society.

☞ We could either bring positive change to society through social action to solve societal issues or pretend like we don't care.

Chapter Five

Practical Steps for Social Action Projects

Chapter Five

Practical Steps for Social Action Projects

It is common knowledge that all communities have one or more problems that we can solve through social action.

In this chapter, I want to encourage you to identify problems, learn how to solve them, and take action to solve them. It is not enough to know that you have skills for social action or that there are problems in society; you must take practical steps to implement your social action projects.

Communities Have Problems, Think Outside The Box

When you look at your community what do you see? Do you see a perfect society where there are no problems or you see one full of problems and pressing needs? Most people because they are engrossed with their jobs at workplace and more so because they are focused on their monthly salaries do not take out time to find out the problems that exist in their communities. If we would take a break from the hustle and bustle of life, from the rat race for survival, we would notice that right beside us are people who are in gross need. If we would care to study our surroundings we would realize that there are problems everywhere looking for who to solve them. It is often the case that we are too egocentric to notice the plight of our neighbours. We are too concerned about ourselves to care about other humans in our society.

There are too many problems in society for anyone to claim ignorance of them. Here are some of the problems in our societies:

☞ Poverty
☞ Homelessness
☞ Gender Inequality
☞ Ethnic Crisis

☞ Mental Health Issue

☞ Lack of Healthcare

☞ Leadership and Political Crisis

☞ Domestic Violence

☞ Alcohol and Drug Addiction

☞ Marital and Relationship problems

☞ Child trafficking

☞ Fraud and Armed robbery

☞ Lack of food and water supply etc.

If we look around, we would see many more problems facing societies and nations. The question is, who will bring a solution to each of these problems?

You Are A Solution Provider

While most people would not give a damn about finding out the problems that exist in their societies, others would notice them, and instead of thinking of how to solve them, resort to complaining and playing the blame game. They would blame the government and point fingers at everyone else as being responsible for solving the problems. If you are such a person that exonerates yourself and feels indifferent about the problems in your society, you are simply ignorant of your role in that society.

We all have but one role to play in society. That is to solve problems and proffer solutions! We exist on earth to solve problems. The reason you were born is not merely to eat, drink, and have pleasure. You were born to solve problems. You do not exist to merely get a job, get married, and have children. You exist to be a solution provider to the problems of mankind. You were created to make a difference in your society and nation. You were born to impact your nation.

"The purpose of life is not to be happy. It is to be useful, to be honorable, to be compassionate, to have it make some difference that you have lived and lived well."

-Ralph Waldo Emerson

I cannot overemphasize the fact that we were

all created and exist to solve problems. You and I are solution providers and unless we take responsibility for solving the problems that plague our communities, those problems will linger and many people would suffer or die as a result of our indifference and negligence. If we act, we would be instrumental in the eradication of such problems. That is exactly what Julia Lalla-Maharajh is doing.

Julia Lalla-Maharajh OBE is the founder and CEO of Orchid Project based in the UK. She became very passionate about the eradication of female genital mutilation (FGM) after she first encountered the issue while volunteering with Voluntary Service Overseas (VSO) in Ethiopia. She returned to the UK and founded Orchid Project, a charity based in London, UK, which has a vision of a world free from FGM[1]

Without Actions Nothing Changes

To effect a change in the community; you

must take action. Most people identify problems and know that they ought to provide solutions to those problems; however, they do nothing to effect positive change. No matter how passionate you are about solving a problem or how quickly you identify those problems, if you do not take action to solve them, nothing will change. Nothing changes until you take action.

"Small deeds done are better than great deeds planned".

-Peter Marshall

To act and bring solutions to societal problems, you must have an algorithm, a plan to follow. I have outlined below the following steps for implementing social action:

☞ **Identify the problems.** What kind of problems are you passionate to solve? What differences or impacts would you like to make? What information have you gathered about the issue?

☞ **Know your target audience.** Who are the people affected by the problems? Study and understand the community or people you want to help.

☞ **Proffer possible solutions.** Learning and researching the problems will help you discern and come up with potential solutions.

☞ **Identify stakeholders.** Seek support and advice from people, organizations, and community groups especially from those who can influence or create a change.

☞ **Set up your working team.** Discuss your project goals and objectives with friends or somebody who will share your vision and be happy to get involved in your social action.

☞ **Form partnership and collaboration.** Seek support from other organizations that are working on similar projects that you could partner with or learn from, including faith-based and community groups.

☞ **Develop an effective action plan for your project.** Define your goals and objectives. Choose practical steps that are specific, measurable, and attainable. Delegate tasks for the rest of your team.

☞ **Implement your action project.** Use your skills, passion, and other resources that you have

☞ **Monitoring and evaluation of your project are very vital**. To do this, you need to ask for feedback from participants and your service users. Keep records, data, and any other document. This will help you to track the results, measure the impacts of your project and know areas to improve on

You will see how I applied each of these steps to my social action projects in subsequent chapters. I do hope that you will apply them while creating your social action project.

Nuggets Five

☞ It is not enough to know that you have skills for social action or that there are problems in society; you must take practical steps to implement your social action projects.

☞ Most people because they are engrossed with their jobs at workplace and also because they are focused on their monthly salaries do not take out time to find out the problems that exist in their communities.

☞ To effect a change in the community; you must take actions.

☞ If we would take a break from the hustle and bustle of life, from the rat race for survival, we would notice that right beside us are people who are in gross need.

☞ If we would care to study our surroundings we would realize that there are problems everywhere looking for who would solve them.

☞ It is often the case that we are too egocentric to notice the plight of our neighbours. We are too concerned about ourselves to care about other humans in our society.

☞ We all have but one role in society. That is to solve problems and proffer solutions! We exist on earth to solve problems.

☞ The reason you were born is not merely to eat, drink, and have pleasure. You were born to solve problems.

☞ You do not exist to merely get a job, get married, and have children. You exist to be a solution provider to the problems of mankind.

☞ You were created to make a difference in your society and nation. You were born to impact your nation.

☞ You and I are solution providers and unless we take responsibility for solving the problems that plague our communities, those problems will linger and many people would suffer or die as a result of our indifference and negligence.

☞ No matter how passionate you are about solving a problem or how quickly you identify those problems, if you do not take action to solve them, nothing will change. Nothing changes until you take action.

Chapter Six

I am a Biomedical Scientist. What are you?

Chapter Six

I am a Biomedical Scientist. What are you?

We all have our different professions and workplace experiences. Being a biomedical scientist, I have dedicated this chapter to promote the importance of biomedical science and also to inspire the younger generations.

If you are thinking about a career choice and you are passionate about helping others and saving lives, biomedical science is one of the caring careers to consider. You may not be a biomedical scientist but I want to challenge you in this chapter to see your profession as a "God-given-calling" and not as a source of income only. I will also show you how you can become a biomedical scientist should you desire to become one.

How And When I Became Interested In Biomedical Science.

As a young high school student, choosing a career path was very challenging. After attending a few career talk events in my school, I started thinking and considering which course to study at the University. As a science student with a passion for healthcare and helping others, I was able to narrow my interests to a few medical courses. Nevertheless, I was still unsure about what specific course to study. I wanted to choose a career that I liked, not what others chose for me!

I used to think that doctors and nurses are the only essential healthcare workers working in the hospital. However, I came to realize that my initial perception was wrong as I later discovered many other essential healthcare workers that are doing different life-saving jobs, whose roles are not well known to the public. Now, let me share with you my experience with one of them.

During my adolescence, I had many experiences of visiting the hospital laboratory for blood tests whenever I was sick. As you know, malaria infection is very common in Africa. Hence, it was always significant for me to visit the hospital for a check-up if I felt unwell. I noticed that my doctor always advised me to go for blood tests so that he could confirm that I had a malaria infection and not something else. He often told me that he would like to see my laboratory test reports before he could prescribe the appropriate medications.

The memory of these past experiences came to my mind at the time I was thinking about career choices. It was these memories that triggered my curiosity about the role of people working in the laboratory. I started asking questions like; Who are these laboratory staff wearing white coats like doctors? What do they do? How lucrative is their job? I got some answers to these questions when I was allowed to partake in a laboratory tour.

Entering into the pathology laboratory for the first time and observing the processing of blood samples by the lab staff was very engrossing. I saw different methods of blood sample collection from patients including the finger-prick for tests like PCV and Malaria. I saw how they performed a urinalysis test and urine culture to detect bacterial infections. For the first time, I examined both positive and negative malaria slides under the microscope. I was also shown around the laboratory and witnessed the process of blood donation by donors and cross-matching of blood for hospital patients. It was this tour that inspired my interest in working in a hospital laboratory. Therefore, biomedical science became one of the career choices I had in mind to study at University. This was how I developed a passion for biomedical science. After high school, I successfully gained admission to study biomedical science at the University College Hospital, Ibadan, Nigeria and I graduated in 1993. After practicing for some years, I relocated to the UK in 2005 to study for a master's degree in biomedical science and to advance my career.

"But whatever path you choose, whatever career you decide to go after, the important thing is that you keep finding joy in what you're doing, especially when the joy isn't finding you."

- Lauren Graham

What is your profession, vocation, or career? If yours is in engineering, education, medicine, business, politics, entertainment, or sports, then see it as your calling or life mission. If you are so passionate about your career, you can initiate a social action project out of it to impact society. I love my job and I will use this chapter of the book to promote my noble profession-Biomedical Science.

What Is Biomedical Science?

Biomedical science is a career in medical

science or modern medicine that deals with the scientific analysis, processing, and testing of body fluid and tissue samples taken or collected from patients by doctors, nurses, or phlebotomists. Biomedical science is also known as Medical Laboratory Sciences in some countries.

The body fluid or tissue samples are sent to the pathology laboratory where biomedical scientists analyze them using a range of tests to identify what type of disease or infection is present. Subsequently, a laboratory test report is produced that will aid the doctor's decisions in the diagnosis, treatment, and management of patient's health conditions.

"Pathology services sit at the heart of patient diagnosis and treatment – in fact 70% of decisions about patient care depend on the results of a test carried out by scientists in a pathology laboratory." - Carter Report 2006

Yes, that is a fact! When you are sick, your

doctor will need to consider your laboratory test report before making any clinical decisions for your treatment. Biomedical scientists have always been essential healthcare workers but there is a very low public recognition of who they are, what they do, and the positive impacts they make in the health sector.

A positive turn around for this profession is that the vital roles of biomedical scientists have now been highlighted to the general public since the beginning of the Coronavirus (Covid-19) health crisis. This recognition is significant because biomedical scientists all over the world are working tirelessly behind the scenes to support the diagnosis, treatment, and management of all the suspected and confirmed patients during the crisis and beyond.

As professionals, we usually work in the pathology laboratories using both fully and semi-automated analyzers in single and different laboratory disciplines which include:

☞ Clinical Biochemistry

☞ Clinical Immunology

☞ Haematology

☞ Virology

☞ Genetics

☞ Molecular Pathology

☞ Blood Transfusion (Blood Bank)

☞ Medical Microbiology

☞ Histopathology / Cellular Pathology

☞ Cytology or Cytopathology

Recently in the UK, the multi-disciplinary practice was introduced into the profession whereby a biomedical scientist is trained to a high level of competency allowing him/her to work across other disciplines as stated below[1]:

⊙ **Blood Sciences**

☞ Clinical Biochemistry

☞ Clinical Immunology

☞ Haematology

☞ Blood Transfusion (Blood Bank)

⊙ **Cell Sciences**

☞ Cytology or Cytopathology

☞ Histopathology / Cellular Pathology

⊙ **Infection Sciences**
- ☞ Virology
- ☞ Medical Microbiology

⊙ **Genetics and Molecular Pathology**
- ☞ Genetics
- ☞ Molecular Pathology

I find my job very fulfilling, it's a service to humanity, and I am passionate about doing it very well to save lives. On the other hand, the role could be very challenging sometimes because, whatever professional decision I make when reporting test results, can impact the lives and well-being of the patients. Therefore, this job role is very sensitive and requires the ability to work under pressure, professionalism, attention to detail, multitasking skills, competence, and excellence on the job.

"Believe passionately in what you do, and never knowingly compromise your standards and values. Act like a true professional, aiming for true excellence, and the money will follow." -David Maister

Haematology and blood transfusion are my specific areas of practice, where I have been saving lives for over 25 years. In haematology, I use automated haematology analyzers to process blood samples to investigate the formation, composition, function, and diseases of the blood. I also microscopically identify abnormalities of different types of blood cells. Few of the diseases diagnosed in Haematology include anaemia, leukaemia, malaria, sickle cell disease, and bleeding disorders such as haemophilia and thrombosis.

My main duties in Blood transfusion include testing for blood grouping, antibody screening, and specific antibody identification. I also crossmatch red cells to ensure that the donor's blood is compatible with the patient's plasma for routine and emergency blood transfusion. Examples of those who require transfusions include trauma patients, cancer patients, surgical patients, and pregnant women. I also provide blood products like

Platelets, Fresh frozen plasma (FFP), Cryoprecipitate, Clotting factor concentrates, and Human albumin solution (HAS) to support patients' treatment. All these I do at work, and I love what I do!

"The only way to do great work is to love what you do. If you haven't found it yet, keep looking. Don't settle." -Steve Jobs

My Daily Workplace Journal

I joined the Liverpool University Hospitals NHS Foundation Trust in Jan 2015, and I work in Haematology and Blood Transfusion laboratory department. This trust covers Aintree Hospital, Royal Liverpool Hospital, and Broadgreen Hospital[2]. The pathology services of these hospitals were merged in 2013 to form a single entity known as Liverpool Clinical Laboratories (LCL), which is the largest pathology service provider in Cheshire and Merseyside[3]

My workplace is a community of dedicated and committed people working together to serve humanity. My colleagues are amazing, I have a good rapport with them and I enjoy working here! I work autonomously across three hospital sites and participate in the 24hrs laboratory services to save and improve the lives of our patients within the hospital and in the community. Now, let me enlighten you on what I do in my workplace.

Start of The Day Shift: 08:30 am

I always aim to get to work before 08:30 am. This allows me time to have a coffee in the staff room before starting my shift and that I start work on time.

During the day, I work either in Haematology and Coagulation sections or Blood transfusion, depending on the daily rota. During the out-of-hours shift, I work across the three sections of the laboratory. Upon starting my day shift, the first thing I do is to take over from the night staff by reading through the shift handover notes as well as having verbal communication with my colleagues to discuss any important issues. These may include outstanding work, patient`s results, or requests for blood products that require immediate action to ensure continuity of service provision. I then ensure that all the analyzers are ready for the day shift by checking that the daily maintenance and morning internal quality control (IQC) samples are processed and passed. I make sure reagents on the analyzers are in date and are sufficient to cover the workload until the next quality control samples are due for processing.

The day shift

Working in Haematology and Coagulation Sections.

Blood samples arrive in the laboratory from a range of locations including the wards, A+E, and GP surgeries. I see real people behind each of these samples; therefore as blood samples arrive, patient's details are thoroughly checked on both the sample and request form, ensuring they meet the laboratory minimum data standard requirements for acceptance, and then labeled up correctly with sample barcode numbers.

They are then immediately booked into the laboratory computer system using Laboratory Information Management System (LIMS) known as Telepath. This part of the sample`s journey is usually completed by medical laboratory assistants during routine hours, but it is the responsibility of all competent staff, including biomedical scientists, during out of hours or times of urgency.

Tests performed in the haematology laboratory include a full blood count (FBC), clotting screen, factor assays, erythrocyte sedimentation rate (ESR), malaria screen, a glandular fever screening test (GFST), sickle cell disease testing, blood film morphology, and any other special tests as requested by the doctor. Samples are processed on fully automated haematology and coagulation analyzers, and the majority of the results are auto authorized by a thought-through system. However, on certain occasions, I may be required to manually review and validate results on the analyzer before the interpretation, authorization, and reporting of results are done on the Telepath.

For some abnormal results, I might need to take necessary actions like checking sample integrity, making and examining a blood film, or simply re-process the sample to correct an obscure result, before reporting the results. For abnormal FBC test results with high white blood cells (WBC) count, I will need to make a blood film and examine the blood morphology microscopically for any abnormal features that might suggest blood cancer like Leukaemia. I will then use both my scientific knowledge and professional judgment to report my findings and take further actions where required. For example, I might need to phone out the results to inform the ward staff, GP, haematology consultant, or referring the sample for further investigations. Any out of range clotting screen and positive malaria test results are phoned to the ward staff for immediate actions. I report blood film morphology for abnormal FBC results by looking at the blood films under a light microscope for morphological features to confirm the diagnose of malaria infection, types of anaemia, bacterial infection, leukaemia, sickle cell disease, and other blood cancers or infections.

Although I do not have direct contact with the hospital patients, I am always patient-focused, acting in their best interest as my job role has a significant impact on their treatment. I prioritize urgent samples from acute locations like haematology clinics, intensive care unit (ICU), theatres, accident, and emergency (A+E) departments so that patient's treatment is not delayed.

The turn-around time for many of these tests is one hour. Checking the overdue and outstanding work list every 30mins is, therefore, essential to ensure any missing samples or tests are identified on time and processed immediately. Working in haematology and coagulation laboratories can be challenging at times due to the high sample workload and working to ensure the turn-around time is always met. I always prioritize my workload and perform my job with a high level of concentration knowing that giving incorrect results could have huge consequences on the patients.

At Lunch Time

Apart from the brief tea breaks of 20mins in the morning and late afternoon, my colleagues and I also take a one-hour lunch break at different times to ensure continuous service provision. The sample workload begins to increase especially after lunchtime as many samples arrive from GP surgeries. Sometimes, the analyzers break down during my shift and I have the responsibility to perform the troubleshooting. If troubleshooting is not successful to fix the analyzers, I have to continue to use other available analyzers to process samples for the rest of the day while I ask for help from my colleagues to fix it or better still, call out the service engineer.

As more and more samples arrive in the laboratory, it can be very challenging to keep on top of the workload. Hence, the prioritization of the workload is very important. I use my organizational and multi-tasking skills to perform different tasks. I use my leadership skills to delegate some tasks to my colleagues so that we can tidy up the workload as much as possible before the end of the shift.

Towards End of The Day Shift.

Towards the end of my shift, there could still be some outstanding work to do, I prioritize in-patient samples and try to complete all the routine work. I ensure urgent results are phoned out to both the wards and GP surgeries when required. The checking of overdue and outstanding worklist continues to identify any tests or samples that are missing. I ensure reagents and any other consumables are replenished for the next shift. I ensure afternoon IQC samples are processed and passed and try to tidy up the workload as much as possible before handing over.

End of Day Shift: 17:00hrs

Before handing over, I write down any important messages on the handover sheet and also give some verbal messages to my colleagues as part of the late shift hand-over. The late shift is from 13:00hrs to 21:00hrs. I inform my colleagues of any outstanding issues or problems with the analyzers that might need resolving or monitoring; or any urgent FBC or clotting screen results and outstanding work that requires immediate attention.

Working in Blood Transfusion Section

Blood transfusion samples are sent to the laboratory from the wards for blood grouping, antibody screening, and sometimes with a request for blood or blood products. Sample receipt and acceptability are a very crucial part of blood transfusion process. So, after receiving these samples, the first thing I do is to check and ensure that patient details on the sample match the request form. This is very important to prevent errors like wrong blood in the tube.

If I identify any errors that do not meet the transfusion acceptance criteria, I reject the sample immediately and inform the ward staff to send a new sample.

Accepted samples are booked in using Telepath and then processed by a fully automated transfusion analyzer which tests the red cells for ABO and RhD antigens while the plasma is tested for antibodies. Occasionally, I do perform manual testing if the analyzer is unable to give definitive results due to various reasons. If the antibody screen is positive, further testing is required in the form of an antibody identification panel, to identify the specific antibody the patient has developed in their plasma. Patients can develop allo-antibodies if they have received a blood transfusion before, if they are currently pregnant or if they have been pregnant before.

Patients can also develop antibodies against their own red cells, in this case, the antibodies are called "auto-antibodies". For the patient's safety, I ensure that antibody identification is performed accurately so that I can select, cross-match, and issue compatible blood to the patient if needed. In a situation where the antibody identification is inconclusive, the sample is sent to the reference laboratory for further investigations.

As requests are coming in, I prioritize my workload, issue red cells and other blood products like platelets, prophylactics anti-D, fresh frozen plasma (FFP) for the patients, and at the same time continue to process samples for grouping and antibody screening. High priority is given to tasks like manual cross-match requests, as this might take a longer time than expected before compatible blood can be issued for the patient. Checking of patient's details is repeatedly done during sample processing, before and after blood units are issued to ensure patients' safety. Before putting the blood units inside the Blood Issue Fridge for collection by ward staff, I ensure to check the patient's details again-this is the final checking.

Working in the transfusion laboratory can be stressful sometimes because of the demanding workload and telephone requests from hospital staff. Any error can affect the patients. To prevent this, I am always proactive in making informed, reasoned, and professional decisions about my practice with attention to detail and by following the laboratory standard operating procedures.

The transfusion team in the laboratory is part of the hospital trauma protocol; this is because we need to be on hand at all times to provide any blood or blood products in the case of an emergency. Hence, the trauma bleep is always carried by me or another colleague of mine. Examples of when the bleep may be activated include a road traffic accident, a fall, a shooting, knife stabbing, etc. If activated, the clinicians often request a major haemorrhage pack which includes 4 units of red cells, 4 units of fresh frozen plasma (FFP), 1 bag of platelets, and sometimes 2 bags of cryoprecipitate may be required. I must provide these products promptly to help save the life of the patient. In emergency conditions like this, I always demonstrate my ability to work under pressure. I ensure clear and timely communication with clinical staffs and my colleagues, this is very vital in blood transfusion laboratory as this can have an impact on safe transfusion practice.

I use my professional judgment to ensure that compatible blood and other blood products are selected and issued within the time frame. Sometimes, the emergency situation can be so stressful but I have developed great experience of working under pressure. I know how to prioritize the tasks and when to ask for help if needed. Knowing the big role I play in saving the life of a trauma patient always makes me feel good!

At Lunch Time

My colleagues and I take a one-hour lunch break at different times to ensure continuous service provision. The transfusion laboratory is always busy; therefore requires a lot of attention to detail and multi-tasking skills. As more samples arrive, I process them along-side antenatal samples for blood grouping and antibody screening. I use my multi-tasking skills to perform different tasks while some tasks are delegated to my colleagues as we work as a team. Sometimes, I take delivery of a new batch of reagents and perform acceptance testing and validation on them before use.

Towards End of The Day Shift

I continue to prioritize my workload, performing manual cross-matching requests, issuing blood, and other blood products as I receive requests from the wards. I answer telephone calls for any enquiries from the wards and other hospitals including National Blood Service. On a few occasions, I might need to order blood for some patients that need special requirements like irradiated products from National Blood Services. I also check the blood bank stock level and take necessary actions.

I ensure afternoon internal control samples are processed and passed. Sometimes, I do have a bad day when the sample flow never stops throughout my shift. This might be very challenging but through experience, I know how to prioritize my workload, how to delegate tasks to others, when to ask for help and when to take tea breaks so that I can be mentally refreshed.

End of Day Shift: 17:00hrs

I tidy up my workload as much as possible. It is very important that information is communicated correctly between shifts, therefore I always write down my important messages on the shift handover book and also give messages by verbal communication while handing-over to the late shift staff. The late shift is from 13:00hrs to 21:00hrs. I inform them of any urgent or outstanding tasks like antibodies identifications, send away samples or manual cross-match requests, or any cause of an existing major hemorrhage that I have dealt with but might still need monitoring.

The start of Night Shift: 20:30hrs

The night or out of hours (OOH) shift is from 20.30hrs to 08.30hrs. This shift involves working as a lone worker across the three sections of the laboratory; routine hematology, coagulation, and blood transfusion. This requires a lot of multi-tasking skills, the ability to prioritize workload, and sometimes working under pressure. While processing all the samples, validating and reporting results, I also receive phone calls from the wards for advice, queries, add-on requests, and request for blood and blood products. I perform my duties with a high level of professionalism. Through my routine practice, I always try to learn something new every day to improve myself and become more skillful on the job, this has helped me to develop a set of valuable and transferable skills that are very useful for my community engagement activities. We are all supposed to transfer the valuable skills we develop from our workplaces to the community and use them to initiate social action projects for the benefit of others.

How To Become A Biomedical Scientist

Are you a hands-on person? Do you love and care for people? If yes, then you will enjoy being a biomedical scientist. You will need to study science subjects in your high school or college with good grades in biology, chemistry, and any other subjects, and then you must gain a BSc degree in biomedical science.

If you study in the UK, your degree must be

accredited by the Institute of Biomedical Science (IBMS) with a period of laboratory placements where you have to complete an IBMS registration training portfolio[4]. This will provide you with all the scientific knowledge and training you require to begin your career. If you study abroad, IBMS membership will give you a great opportunity to develop knowledge, skills, experience and to advance your career[5]

Regardless of the country where you have your degree, for you to practice in the UK as a biomedical scientist, it's legally required of you to be registered and licensed by the Health and Care Professions Council (HCPC) to protect the safety of the public. If you have your training outside the UK like me, your HCPC registration will be processed through the international application route.

Don't confuse IBMS with HCPC, they are two different bodies. IBMS is the professional body for biomedical scientists only while HCPC is the statutory regulatory body for biomedical scientists and many other healthcare professions in the UK. You will need to maintain the standards of proficiency and continuing professional development (CPD) with these bodies at all times.

Biomedical Science Career Prospects

Believe me, biomedical science is a lucrative and high demand career anywhere in the world. Many biomedical science graduates get jobs in various employment sectors while some proceed to postgraduate studies. In the UK, the majority of them get jobs in the pathology laboratories of National Health Service (NHS) hospitals and NHS Blood and Transplant (NHSBT).

 Many also find jobs with the private hospitals and pathology laboratories while others get their fulfilling jobs in other sectors which include:

> ☞ Academic departments in the university as lecturers

☞ Pharmaceutical and Biotechnology companies

☞ Infection Control/ Forensics laboratories

☞ Government Advisory and professional body sectors

☞ Public Health sector

☞ Monitoring Drugs and Therapy companies

☞ Veterinary Diagnostic Services

☞ Research and Quality assurance sectors

I strongly believe this chapter gave you some insightful information about the important role of biomedical scientists in the healthcare sector.

I am a biomedical scientist, what are you? I want you to know that your profession is as important as mine. I implore you to give the same diligence, excellence, and service at your workplace like I am doing at mine. It doesn't matter whether you are a lawyer, an engineer, a teacher, an accountant, a taxi driver, or a cleaner; one thing is true; you are called to serve humanity with your skills. Together, through the dignity of labour we can change the world and bring solutions to the problems that plague mankind.

Nuggets Six

☞ No matter what your profession is; engineering, education, medicine, business, politics, entertainment, or sports, see it as your calling or life mission.

☞ If you are so passionate about your career, initiate a social action project out of it to impact society.

☞ We are all supposed to transfer the valuable skills we develop from our work experience to our community in the form of community development projects.

☞ It doesn't matter whether you are a lawyer, an engineer, a teacher, an accountant, a taxi driver, or a cleaner; one thing is true; you are called to serve humanity with your skills.

Chapter Seven

Insights from My Social Action Projects

Chapter Seven

<u>Insights from My Social Action Projects</u>

"Social action, just like physical action, is steered by perception"-Kurt Lewin

In this chapter, I am going to share my experiences from the community engagements through my participation in different social action projects. As stated earlier, social action project is about you identifying issues or problems in the community, learning about them, and bringing about potential solutions to solve them. This could be in form of any activity, initiative, event, or program to positively impact the lives of people or the community. It can be as little as providing the right information or mentorship to individuals that will improve their lives. It can also be as large as setting up a non-governmental organization, charities, charitable foundations, or social enterprise to create positive social impacts in society.

In 2012, I became more active within my community after my wife and I were inspired to start PathLab Support, a social enterprise with the intention to support sick people, most especially individuals and families affected with Sickle Cell Disease in the UK and Nigeria. PathLab Support has now become a platform for a few other social action projects including Blood Donation Campaign which is an action taken to address one of the national health issues in the UK - shortage of blood donors from Black, Asian, and Minority Ethnic (BAME) communities.

"To turn caring into action, we need to see a problem, find a solution and deliver impact" -Bill Gates

Sickle Cell Disease Awareness Campaign

I am so passionate about Sickle Cell Disease (SCD) awareness campaign because of my personal experience and desire to make my little contributions to end this global health problem. This life-threatening disease commonly affects people of African, Caribbean, Middle-Eastern, Asian, and Mediterranean origin; however, migration and racial marriages have raised the prevalence in almost every nation of the world.

My wife and I were born and raised in Nigeria, West Africa, where the prevalence of SCD is very high. We met at the university where we were both classmates and course mates. We started dating in 1992, a year before we both graduated. We later discovered that we are both sickle cell carriers (HbAS), though we made a few attempts to break off the courtship we eventually got married.

Partners like ours are at a very high risk of having their unborn children affected with the severe form of this disease which is Sickle Cell Anaemia –HbSS. Scientifically; there is a 25% chance or probability for every pregnancy that the baby will be affected.

In our own case, we were three times lucky! Yes, three times by miracle or by luck because we have three children and none of them has HbSS. This is very rare! It was this experience that inspired us of doing something for others. As a way of giving back to the community, we started promoting public awareness of SCD and also provide any form of support to affected individuals and families.

"Other people are going to find healing in your wounds. Your greatest life messages and your most effective ministry will come out of your deepest hurts" -Rick Warren

SCD is the most common and fastest-growing genetic blood disorder in the UK[1]. Approximately, 15,000 people are living with this condition, 240,000 people are healthy carriers and 300 babies are born every year with SCD[2]. Immigration into the UK and new births are causing an increase in the prevalence. Therefore to reduce the prevalence of this disease, a continuous public awareness campaign is necessary.

As a Sickle Cell Advocate, I have been actively raising public awareness for the past few years. I do this through workshops and seminars, educating people especially young and unmarried. I work in partnership with charities like Liverpool Sickle Cell and Thalassaemia Support Group (LSTG) as I take my campaign to different community groups and faith-based organizations. I also advocate for social support for affected individuals and families most especially those living in Africa.

It's very interesting how I always link my workplace experience of testing people's blood for SCD with raising the awareness of SCD and blood donation to highlight reasons why SCD prevention is very necessary. In my campaign presentations, I always highlight the following:

☞ SCD is preventable! Prevention is better than treatment or cure.

☞ The only possible cure for this disorder is a bone marrow transplant.

☞ If you are single and unmarried, knowing your sickle cell or Hb genotype status before pregnancy or any serious relationship is very important.

☞ If you discover that you are a sickle cell carrier-HbAS, make sure you know your partner's Hb genotype or sickle cell status as well.

☞ Sickle Cell Anaemia-HbSS is inherited from both parents who are carriers of the sickle cell gene, which is one gene from each parent or partner.

☞ There is a 25% chance or probability for every pregnancy that the unborn baby will be affected.

☞ People living with Sickle Cell Anaemia-HbSS depend on regular blood transfusion to survive.

☞ Sickle Cell Anaemia-HbSS will put a psycho-social and financial burden on affected individuals and families.

☞ For partners at risk, seeking knowledge, information, and attending genetic counseling will help you know your possible options and empower you to make an informed decision.

The Impact

More and more people in my community are being informed with in-depth knowledge of SCD and the consequences or the risks of taking chances. Affected individuals and families are being empowered on how to look after their health and wellbeing through counselling and peer support group meetings.

Also, young and unmarried people are becoming more aware of the importance of taking a blood test to know their sickle cell status before any serious relationship or pregnancy. Finally, SCD prevention in our communities will reduce the burden of treatment costs on our National Health Service (NHS).

Hospital Outreach To Africa

One of the objectives of PathLab Support is supporting the sick, especially those affected with sickle cell anaemia in the UK and Africa. With the objective in mind, we introduced our support initiative for sick children to the management of University College Hospital (UCH), Ibadan Nigeria, West Africa. This initiative was welcomed by the hospital management, and this led to a partnership agreement between PathLab Support and UCH in February 2012. Since then, we have been helping children on hospital admission to off-set their hospital bills.

Apart from financial support, we also support the sick through hospital visits with the donation of gift items. Our first hospital outreach to Nigeria was in 2013, which was to UCH, Oluyoro Catholic Hospital, Oni, and Son Memorial hospital, all based in the city of

Ibadan. For this outreach, we organized a charity collection of brand new toys/gift items from many Liverpool based families, friends and colleagues. This initiative was also supported by few McDonald Restaurants here in the city of Liverpool, as they donated their happy meal toys to us to support the outreach.

For smooth logistic purposes, the outreach was planned in collaborations with The Bridge Network, a faith-based organization in the city of Ibadan. The outreach dates and time were also planned and agreed upon with the management of these three hospitals. All donated gift items were shipped to Nigeria, my wife and I also travelled to join the lovely team from The Bridge Network. During this first hospital visit, we reached out to over 300 children in three different hospitals with our gift items, putting smiles on their faces. After 2013, we also organised similar outreach in December 2014 and December 2019.

The Impact

Many children were able to attend their monthly hospital check-ups and receive treatments through our financial support. We have put smiles on the faces of over 1,000 children on hospital beds through our hospital outreach and gifts donation.

Both the children and their parents were very happy and grateful that people from thousand of miles away were thinking about them. This hospital outreach had positive feelings and emotions on the children and helped their journey to recovery. We received feedback that the children felt much better after each visit.

Children's Hospital Christmas Visit

Alder Hey Children's NHS Foundation Trust is located in Liverpool, a beautiful city where I have lived for more than 10 years. This hospital is one of the largest children's hospitals in the UK that cares and treats over 330,000 children and young people every year for different life-threatening health conditions. The current site, the new state-of-the-art Alder Hey hospital complex was built and opened for public use in October 2015.

When I heard about the opening, I was so excited to do something remarkable and to give back to the hospital where my family had once benefited from. After I researched what the hospital was collecting and specific items they wanted people to give to the children, I came up with an initiative to organise a charity collection of new toys, gift items, and cash donations in my workplace to support the children in the hospital admission. This initiative was welcomed and supported by my colleagues within my workplace community, which is Liverpool Clinical Laboratory (LCL), the pathology service provider for Royal Liverpool, Aintree, and Broadgreen hospitals.

For proper documentation, a few of my colleagues in each of the pathology laboratories across the three hospital sites volunteered to assist me to monitor the fundraising, collection of new toys and other gift items for a period of two months. I had already liaised with the charity department of the hospital about this initiative and the proposed visit. Apart from the 63 brand new toys donated, we also raised £510 in cash. This money was used to purchase additional 25 toys. On Saturday, 12th December 2015, a group of excited people from my workplace community (LCL) wearing their Christmas jumpers, visited the new hospital site to give back to the hospital that we and our families had once benefited from.

The Impact

We were given a tour around the new hospital complex as we made the 2015 Christmas season very special for the children on hospital beds by putting smiles on their faces through the donation of 88 toys/gift items. This hospital visit had positive feelings and emotions on the children and helped their journey to recovery.

STEM Ambassador Volunteering

In October 2015, my son who was in primary school then came home one day with a letter from his teacher. The school was planning a one-week event called "Aspire and Achieve Week". The week was designed to get pupils thinking about their future aspirations and to enable them to have an insight into the types of jobs they can do when they become older.

So, parents were invited to come and talk about their workplaces and the jobs they do. I indicated my interest and I was given a slot for that week. I remember that I wore my white Lab coat while giving my little presentation about my workplace and the job I do, which was very exciting.

This experience inspired me to know how giving a brief career talk can make a big difference in the lives of young people. I later joined STEM Ambassador program. This program is a nationwide campaign in the UK to encourage young people to develop an interest in and study Science, Technology, Engineering, and Mathematics (STEM) subjects. The campaign also addresses the inadequate number of skilled teachers to teach these subjects. By becoming a STEM Ambassador, you can play a crucial role in inspiring young people with STEM-related subjects and careers[3].

As an ambassador, I use my free time, career, and other workplace transferable skills to engage with many young people between 5-18 years old to promote STEM subjects through activities like presentations, career talk, networking, and mentoring in a few schools. I inspire young people to picture what is like to work in any STEM-related and possible career pathways. I have the opportunity to mentor a few young people within my community as many of them look up to me as their role model.

Through this voluntary role, I use my career skills to inspire the next generation of biomedical scientists. I talk to young people who might not know a lot about my job roles or those who want to know if biomedical science would be a good career path for them. Events like Biomedical Science Day and National Pathology Week are great opportunities for me to engage with young minds and share the enthusiasm and passion that I have for my career.

"Mentoring is passion for skills and knowledge-transfer to young people" - *Lailah Gifty Akita*

Your profession may not be from STEM backgrounds but if you are so passionate about your profession, you can inspire young people to start thinking about that profession, as many of them don't have any idea of what to do when they grow up. You can be a great career mentor and a role model to them in your community by engaging with them in and out of the classroom using your passion, time, and career experiences. You can also support them with things like exam preparations, interview skills, and CV writing.

The Impact

STEM awareness is helping many young people to develop genuine interest and aspirations in science subjects. Many college students are also being inspired to pursue careers in STEM-related courses at the university level including teaching career in science subjects; this will lead to more young people showing interest in post-graduate clinical researches. If we can have more young people today pursuing teaching careers in STEM subjects, then in the nearest future the issue of an inadequate number of skilled teachers to teach science subjects will be addressed.

Hospital Chaplaincy Volunteering

One of the best ways to use your free time is to serve others. Serving people is serving God. Loving people is loving God. There are many good causes and volunteering opportunities through which you can serve and show love to people. I have always been passionate about helping the sick. I see the opportunity to develop this passion more through hospital chaplaincy. I became a volunteer in April 2015 at the same Royal hospital where I work as a biomedical scientist.

Sickness is one of the challenges of life that we will all face at some points. I have been admitted to the hospital for medical treatment a few times before, so I know how isolating and worrying this can be for anybody. Feeling sick and being admitted to the hospital will make anyone unhappy as this will raise all kinds of questions, anxiety, and fears. Hospital admissions will keep you away from your family members, friends, and affect your routine life which could lead to a kind of depression. To alleviate these problems, hospital chaplaincy is there to provide both holistic and pastoral care for patients and their relatives to cope with the psychological, social, and spiritual aspects of their illness and injury.

The chaplaincy also provides emotional and spiritual support for bereaved family members. They also provide support for hospital staff who might be exposed to trauma within the hospital setting.

"Chaplains are missionaries, the human face of Christ, the church that has left the building. We can all be involved in chaplaincy"-Rev. Martyn Atkins

My Day as a Chaplaincy Volunteer

Being a chaplaincy volunteer, I am part of a team that supports the lead chaplain. Before going into the wards, I must report first to the chaplaincy office to collect the list of the patients who requested support from the chaplaincy. This list is often collated and sent to us by the ward staff. I also check our answered phone for any patient referrals by the ward staff or patient's relatives. By checking through the lists, it's easier for me to know who to visit and which ward to go to as each volunteer is allocated to different wards, but I love visiting haematology wards.

After brief prayers and meditations, I go to the wards with the list and my volunteer ID badge. I make sure I sanitize my hands with alcohol hand sanitizer before entering into the wards, also during and after leaving. After greeting and chatting briefly with the ward staff, I then start my job by walking up to the bedside of the first patient on my list. I introduce myself, ask if they will like to talk, and then begin the conversations. While some of them may not be in the mood to talk, many always welcome the conversations as they are willing to share their fears and anxiety with somebody from the chaplaincy. I therefore always listen more, talk less, and allow them to express themselves. Most times, the conversations show their pains, sorrows, and desire for answers to many questions triggered by their sicknesses.

Questions like; Why is this happening to me?

Where is God in this?

It is during the conversations that I know if the patient is identified with any particular faith or not. I do not say any prayers or read the bible passages until they ask for it. I have been trained to be sensitive to patients who may not identify with my faith or any other particular faith. Sometimes, without words, I will just be silent and be there for the patients.

"I was naked and you clothed Me, I was sick and you visited Me, I was in prison and you came to Me" -Jesus Christ, The Bible

Many find hope and assurance during the conversations while many connect with God through their religious faith and belief system for divine healing as they request prayers. After the visit, I always report back to the chaplaincy office to write my reports or feedback. Sometimes I do request the lead chaplain to follow up my patients who might need further help.

Apart from visiting the wards, I also go to the hospital chapel to support patients, staff, and the rest of the chaplaincy team. This is what I love to do, helping people! I use my free time to give hope and assurance to people in hopeless situations. I get great satisfaction and fulfillment from helping out to support the sick.

Are you a caring person and a good listener? Are you empathetic? Are you able to relate well with people? If yes, you too can make a difference by becoming a hospital chaplaincy volunteer. You will be trained to use the sense of your belief system as a Christian, Jewish, Muslim to support patients' faith to enable them to cope with their sickness.

Anybody from any religious or cultural background can be a chaplaincy volunteer; you don't need to be an ordained or professional religious leader. But if you want to be a professional chaplain, you will need to have some religious experiences and professional training or qualifications.

I must say this to you; chaplaincy is not about

converting people to your own faith or belief system. ***Hospital chaplaincy is about showing love, kindness, compassion to patients and supporting them during their health crisis.*** Prison chaplaincy volunteering is another great opportunity you can consider to show love, to offer hope, assurance, and spiritual care to the broken-hearted.

The Impact

Patients always feel loved when they see non-relatives visiting them. Their feeling of loneliness is reduced to a minimal level because of the caring and compassionate people from the chaplaincy. Hospital visits always have positive feelings or emotions on patients and aid their journey to recovery. Many get help to connect with God through their faith and religious belief to manage and overcome their health crisis.

Blood Donation Campaign

Working in the hospital blood transfusion laboratory (Blood bank) allows me to see on daily basis the positive impacts of *"heroic and life-saving act"* of voluntary blood donors. I see the *"miracle"* of blood transfusion; how it improves and saves the lives of many hospital patients.

However, I also see how the shortage of blood donors from Black, Asian, and Minority Ethnic (BAME) communities makes it harder to find the best-matched blood (*blood from donor of same or similar ethnic background as the recipient*) to treat patients affected with Sickle Cell Anaemia (HbSS) and Thalassaemia. These blood disorders are common with people from BAME communities and the affected individuals are blood transfusion-dependent to stay alive. However, due to the shortage of the best-matched blood, these disorders are often treated with regular blood, which puts patients at risk of developing specific blood antibodies that could have been prevented by the use of best-matched blood. The shortage of blood donors from BAME communities is one of the national health-related problems in the UK, and there is a nationwide campaign to tackle this problem[4]. It was my daily work experience in blood transfusion laboratory that inspired me to initiate a local campaign to effect change in my community.

The first thing I did before I started my campaign was that I arranged to meet with the manager of Liverpool Blood Donor Center, located on Dale Street. During the meeting with her and another member of her team, I informed them about my current Sickle Cell Disease awareness campaign. I also discussed my passion, the objectives, action plans for this new project, and my intention to organize community blood drives as one of the ways to encourage people from my community to give blood, most especially those giving blood for the first time.

The meeting was successful as they gave me appropriate advice and information on available tools and resources for the campaign.   A couple of weeks after, I received an email letter dated Wed, 26th Nov

2015 from Theo Clarke, who was then the NHSBT National BAME Marketing Manager, but now the National Proposition and Conversion Manager, expressing his support for my campaign. He wrote and I quote *"This letter is to confirm my support for PathLab Support's excellent work. NHS Blood and Transplant (NHSBT) are committed to continuing with our work within the Black communities to raise awareness of the need for more blood donors to step forward from the Black communities. Central to this work is better working with community groups, organizations, and charities such as PathLab Support.*

We very much welcome working relationships such as this to help NHSBT in our quest to increase the number of Black donors joining the register and to raise awareness of the link between blood donation and Sickle Cell patients.

It is incredibly important that Sickle Cell patients get the best-matched blood possible and one of the best ways to get that match is using blood from a similar ethnic background. As the majority of Sickle Cell patients are of Black heritage, it's really important that we have more Black donors. By informing people about the link between Sickle Cell Disease and blood donation, PathLab Support can make a real difference.

I look forward to hearing how PathLab Support continues to raise awareness and should you need to speak to myself or get advice from NHSBT, please feel free to contact me. Please do also get in touch with any ideas you may have for working together"

To be honest, I wasn't expecting such massive support like this, however, the letter was encouraging and delightful. It highlighted the campaign messages and it was very useful each time I approached my community leaders to seek their support for the campaign.

After putting all the action plan strategies in place, my local campaign was launched in

April 2016 with the very first blood donation awareness workshop. This event was hosted and supported by Love Assembly Discovery Centre (LADC), a faith-based and community organization.

Since then; my team and I have been actively working, promoting the importance of giving blood and also recruiting new blood donors from the BAME communities in Liverpool which include Pakistani, Nigerian, Somali, and other communities including the Caucasian.

My team and I worked with different community groups, faith-based organizations, and other charities like Liverpool Sickle Cell and Thalassaemia Support Group across the city to make a difference. You can't do it all alone and by yourself, collaborations with others make your project goals achievable, easier and faster. We collaborated with a group of faith-based organizations during the annual community fun-day event tagged 'Love Knotty Ash'. We had our campaign stall during this event to promote the importance of giving blood. We were able to answer questions from the audience who came to our stall and we signed up some people as blood donors. We also partnered with different event organizers during their business exhibition and community events like; Pacesetters Business Expo, African Art Exhibitions, Passion For African Fashion (PAFASH), and Global Cultural Day, where we promoted the importance of giving blood and signed up some people as new blood donors.

In June 2019, my team and I had our blood donation campaign stall at Africa Oye music festival. Africa Oye is the UK's largest free celebration of African music and culture, a two-day event holding yearly in the city of Liverpool which attracts over 40,000 people from different ethnic and community backgrounds from all over the UK. While dancing to a variety of music and having fun, we promoted the importance of giving blood, enlightened people who came to our stall, and recruited new blood donors. If you want to make social impacts; you need to socialize!

This was our biggest campaign ever, as we signed up over 100 people as new blood donors in two days. It was amazing! My knowledge and experience of working in the blood transfusion laboratory was an added advantage for me to engage with the audience, most especially when answering their questions and responding to any other enquiries related to blood, blood products, and blood transfusion.

Many of my community leaders did not only welcome and support this campaign; they actively discussed and addressed the negative impact of religious beliefs and cultural barriers to blood donation. A few of them inspired their members by becoming registered blood donors and started giving blood. From the start of this campaign till now, we have given out over 1,000 donor enrolment forms to people at various events across the city as we encouraged them to sign up as blood donors. Also with the support of Liverpool Blood

Donor Centre and the working relationship with NHSBT, we organised a "community blood drive" at two separate times to encourage people to give blood.

Key Facts About Blood Donation

☞ Blood donation is an act of humanity.

☞ 1 in 4 people will need a blood transfusion at some point in their lives

☞ If you are willing to receive blood transfusion tomorrow in case you need it, then you should be willing to give blood today.

☞ Blood donation is one of the ways to give back to your community.

☞ Blood cannot be manufactured; it can only come from voluntary blood donors like you.

☞ If you have Sickle Cell trait (HbAS), you can still give blood in the UK

☞ Blood from donors with a similar ethnic background as the patient gives the best match and outcomes in the long term for the patients.

☞ There is an increase in demand for some rare blood types that are more common in people of black heritage; hence more blood donors are needed from BAME communities.

☞ An average adult has around 10pints of blood, blood donation takes about 1pint from you, after which your body can replace all the cells and fluids that you have lost.

☞ Each time you donate blood, you are improving or saving the lives of 3 people because your whole blood is separated into 3 blood components; red cells, platelets, and plasma. Each of these components is transfused to different patients according to their medical needs.

The Impact

The religious beliefs and cultural barriers to blood donation within my community are gradually being broken down because more and more people from BAME communities in

Liverpool are not only becoming aware of the importance of giving blood but they are also donating blood to save lives. Within the period of four years that this campaign was launched, my team and I have inspired and recruited about 600 people as blood donors from both the BAME and Caucasian communities.

This blood donor recruitment will have a positive impact on our NHS hospitals as this will lead to the constant availability of blood and blood products to meet the needs of all patients especially patients affected with Sickle Cell Disease and Thalassaemia. Having said that, a continuous campaign is needed to encourage more people from the BAME communities to sign up and give blood.

Dear reader, look around your community, you would find one or two areas where you can help and bring a solution to the prevailing problems that people face in that community. Use your workplace skills, your social skills, your ethical skills, your life skills, and your passion to serve your community. You were created to serve and impact your community and nation, don't neglect those who need your service. Go and impact your world!

Nuggets Seven

☞ One of the best ways to use your free or leisure time is to serve others. Serving people is serving God. Loving people is loving God.

☞ Use your workplace skills, your social skills, your ethical skills, your life skills to serve your community.

☞ You were created to serve and impact your community and nation.

☞ You can't do it all alone and by yourself, collaborations with others make your project goals achievable, easier and faster.

☞ Don't neglect those who need your service. Go and impact your world!

☞ If you want to make social impacts; you need to socialize.

Chapter Eight

When Would You Start Your Own Community Project / NGO?

Chapter Eight

When Would You Start Your Own Community Project / NGO?

"You don't have to be great to start, but you have to start to be great". -Zig Ziglar

In this chapter, I want to challenge you to apply all that you have learned in this book to your life and through it create your community project.

Start Now: Your Community Is Waiting For You

You have read about my social action projects and those of others in this book. What has this book inspired you to do for others? What are you going to do for your community? Your community is waiting for you to bring solutions to the problems that plague it. You cannot afford to fail or disappoint them. There is no room for procrastination; now is the time to start.

"The best time to plant a tree was 20 years ago. The second best time is now" -Chinese proverb.

Most people spend their whole life contemplating and procrastinating what to do with their lives and die eventually without doing anything. You don't want to be in that category. You may be thinking that you have enough time to start your social action project and impact your community. But I want you to know that the best time to start is now. Do not live as if you have forever to effect change. No! You have but only today, so start now.

"Nobody makes a greater mistake than he who did nothing because he could do only a little"-Edmund Burke

To accomplish your community project instead of merely wishing and procrastinating, you must do the following:

☞ Start where you are.

☞ Start with what you have; use
your passion, kindness, skill
sets, and other resources that
you have.

☞ Set up and register your
organization; this could be in
form of a social enterprise,
foundation, community group,
charities, or an NGO after a
good cause you are passionate
about.

☞ Start making a difference and
building your legacy.

When ElsaMarie saw the need to start her
social action project, she did not procrastinate
or wish someone else will bring a solution to
the problem. She acted!

ElsaMarie D'Silva is the founder and CEO of
Red Dot Foundation, India. She was a former
aviation professional but later founded Red
Dot Foundation India, a social enterprise that
runs SafeCity App to track reports of sexual
violence and harassment with objectives to

tackle the problem. Since 2012 when SafeCity App was launched, it has been making big differences on the issue of sexual violence in India, Nepal, Kenya, and Cameroon.

She said "About five and a half years ago, I was in the aviation sector. I was working with one of India's largest airlines as vice president - network planning, where I planned the route network. And then, we had this horrific gang rape of a young woman on a bus in Delhi. I'm sure you must have heard about it because it made global news. And that incident was a catalyst for me to decide to quit my job and focus on sexual violence prevention"[1]

What did you notice from the story above? Urgency! When ElsaMarie noticed the problem, she didn't hesitate or procrastinate, she resigned from her job and started a social action project to address it. You may not have to quit your job as she did, but you can start doing something immediately to solve the problems that you have noticed in your society by creating a social action project.

Start now, your community is waiting for you!

What Will Be Your Legacy?

Before bringing the chapter to a close, I want to implore you to live more for legacy than for the mundane things of this world. Money and power are all good but in the end, what matters is the legacy that we leave behind for generations to come. When it's all said and done, we would all be remembered not for the number of houses, cars, academic certificates that we had but for the problems that we solved, the communities we reformed, the down and out that we lifted, the homeless that we sheltered and the lives that we impacted. The only way to live forever is to spend one's life in the service of others. That was exactly what Dr. Hawa Abdi did.

Dr. Hawa Abdi is from Somalia. In the early 1990s during the civil war in Somalia, she set up a clinic and used her career skills to help the vulnerable and save many lives. She also set up schools for the displaced children and orphans.[2] That is a legacy that she created and generations to come will hear of her works. Whenever the history of the civil war is discussed, Dr. Hawa's name and her work would come to mind.

You too can create your legacy, something that generations after you would hear about or benefit from and be glad that someone like you exists or existed. Do you want to be remembered after you are gone from this world? If yes, then start impacting your world, start serving your community, and bringing positive change. What legacy will you leave behind? What will the world remember you for?

"I long to accomplish a great and noble task, but it is my chief duty to accomplish small tasks as if they were great and noble"
-Helen Keller

Conclusion

So much has been said about the need to take your work experience and skills beyond your workplace into your community to effect a change. You have read about different examples of people who are changing the world through social actions and I have highlighted the practical steps you need to start your social action project. The ball is now in your court to take what you have learned and apply it to create your community project and start changing the world right from where you are. Remember, that work is a tool to serve mankind and solve the problems in society. It is time to contribute your quota to make the world a better place. Your skills, experience, money, passion, and everything you have are tools to transform your society and nation. The world is waiting for you. No more egocentrism, it is time to change the world. You were created for impact, for service and to be a blessing to your world. Go and effect a change! Go and create a legacy! Go and solve a problem!

Nuggets Eight

☞ Money, power, and career excellence are all good but in the end, what matters is the legacy that we leave behind for generations to come.

☞ When it's all said and done, we would all be remembered not for the number of houses, cars, academic certificates that we had but for the problems that we solved, the communities we reformed, the down and out that we lifted, the homeless that we sheltered and the lives that we impacted.

☞ You were created for impact, for service and to be a blessing to your world. Go and effect a change! Go and create a legacy! Go and solve a problem!

☞ Your legacy shouldn't be for making a living. Your legacy should be for making a difference.

☞ We are not meant to keep all we receive; not meant to live for ourselves but others.

<u>Reference</u>

Chapter One

1. *https://www.bahai.org/beliefs/life-spirit/*
2. *https://www.gordon.edu/article.cfm?i ArticleID=998*
3. *https://www.history.com/topics/amer ican-revolution/benjamin-franklin*
4. *https://sundayadelajablog.com/excell ence-your-key-to-elevation-part-1/*
5. *https://www.fox5dc.com/news/high-school-student-gives-free-haircuts-to-homeless*
6. *https://edition.cnn.com/2019/10/03/af rica/dr-sulaiman-free-surgeries-intl/index.html*

Chapter Two

1. *https://www.gov.uk/government/publ ications/centre-for-social-action/centre-for-social-action*
2. *Website (In Swedish and English): https://viddinsida.nu/*
3. *https://oxfamblogs.org/fp2p/authors/ maureen-muketha/*
4. *https://foodtank.com/news/tag/tule-vyema/*
5. *https://conversational-leadership.net/community/*

Chapter Three

1. *https://vanderbiltpoliticalreview.com /876/world/i-am-malala-a-battle-cry-for-justice/*
2. *https://slum2school.wordpress.com/f ounder/*
3. *https://www.wral.com/education-in-one-nigerian-slum-goes-digital-as-charity-creates-virtual-learning-hub/19199407/*

4. *https://m.okadabooks.com/book/read er/16470/7?is_preview=yes*

Chapter Four

1. *https://www.goodthingsfoundation.o rg/*
2. *https://www.verywellfamily.com/seve n-social-skills-for-kids-4589865*
3. *https://www.skillsyouneed.com/gener al/life-skills.html*
4. *https://www.thereporterethiopia.com /article/moral-decadence-and-its-impact-society*

Chapter Five

1. *https://www.orchidproject.org/*

Chapter Six

1. *https://careers.ibms.org/discover -biomedical-science/what-is-biomedical-science/*
2. *https://www.liverpoolft.nhs.uk/*

3. *https://www.liverpoolcl.nhs.uk/about-lcl/*
4. *https://www.abdn.ac.uk/careers/resources/documents/5354.pdf*
5. *https://www.ibms.org/join/overseas-applicants/*

Chapter Seven

1. https://www.gov.uk/guidance/sickle-cell-and-thalassaemia-screening-programme-overview
2. *https://www.nice.org.uk/guidance/qs58/documents/nice-standard-urges-healthcare-professionals-to-improve-care-for-people-experiencing-painful-sickle-cell-episodes*
3. *https://www.stem.org.uk/stem-ambassadors*
4. *https://www.blood.co.uk/*

Chapter Eight

1. *https://reddotfoundation.org/*
2. *https://safecity.in/*
3. *https://face2faceafrica.com/article/the-heroic-hawa-abdi-one-of-somalias-first-female-obstetricians-who-saved-thousands-during-the-civil-war*

Printed in Poland
by Amazon Fulfillment
Poland Sp. z o.o., Wrocław

64868608R00125